A Dash c

A DASH O' DORIC

THE WIT AND WISDOM OF THE NORTH-EAST

ROBBIE SHEPHERD
AND NORMAN HARPER

ILLUSTRATED BY GRAHAM MACLENNAN

This edition published in 2001 by
Birlinn Limited
8 Canongate Venture
5 New Street
Edinburgh
EH8 8BH

www.birlinn.co.uk

Copyright © Robbie Shepherd and
Norman Harper 1995

First published in Great Britain in 1995 by
Canongate Books Ltd, Edinburgh
Reprinted in 1996 (twice) and 1998

The right of Robbie Shepherd and Norman Harper
to be identified as the authors of this work has
been asserted by them in accordance with the
Copyright, Designs and Patents Act 1988

All rights reserved. No part of this publication may be
reproduced, stored, or transmitted in any form, or by
any means, electronic, mechanical or photocopying,
recording or otherwise, without the express written
permission of the publisher.

ISBN 1 84158 148 8

British Library Cataloguing-in-Publication Data
A catalogue record for this book is available
from the British Library

Printed and bound by Omnia Books Limited, Glasgow

Contents

Foreword

WHEN WE began the research for this book, we thought that, time permitting, we might take a wee detour and see how far back in the annals of humour we could trace a distinctive North-east of Scotland voice. What began as a passing notion became more of a challenge than we realised and, very soon, our plan to investigate the humour of the North-east took a temporary second place to our determination to delve as far back as possible. Anyone who has traced their family tree will be familiar with the problems that we encountered very quickly. After two or three generations, the leads tease out into myriad combinations and permutations, most of which turn out to be dead ends and are extremely frustrating. But we had an ace in our hand.

We were helped greatly by the archives of the *Press and Journal*. The *P&J* is blessed with one of the fullest records and one of the most fascinating vaults of Scottish history. Although it was not catalogued or cross-referenced in any formal way until the early 1950s, the sheer richness of the material available – all the way back to December, 1747 – makes it surprisingly easy to pick up little nuggets.

Finally, we came to the conclusion that the earliest recorded example of the humour of the North-east comes not from the turn of this century, nor even the turn of the previous one, but from almost 230 years ago.

It involves no less a figure than Dr Samuel Johnson, of Johnson and Boswell fame, the man who once described the noblest prospect in Scotland as being the road to England. Dr Johnson, ('author of the English Dictionary, rambler and idler' records an Aberdeen's *Journal* of September, 1773), was visiting Aberdeen and had been distinctly less than impressed with the 'rudeness of domicile' and the 'coarseness of fellow' he had encountered.

Today, such a newspaper item would be known as 'a

colour piece' – a feature which reports very little hard news but, rather, paints an impression of an event, or a person in the news for other reasons. Only in the last 50 years have most daily newspapers favoured the colour piece, so Aberdeen's *Journal* was clearly far ahead of its time.

It was here that we reached our goal.

The journalist who had been assigned to accompany Dr Johnson on his visit noted that the good doctor had been walking down one of Aberdeen's streets when he came upon a labourer doing his best to harl the side of one of the town's grander houses in the Broadgate. With an array of buckets, tools, mounds of stones and slabs around the workman, Dr Johnson had no option but to step out into the dirt, dubs and dung of the roadway. As he passed the workman and picked his way through the mire, he vented his spleen with what he imagined was some telling sarcasm.

'Good fellow,' he said. 'I trust that the impact of my person did not incommode your labour.'

We can imagine the wee Aberdonian labourer looking up at the bewigged Englishman, in all his velvet finery, and sizing him up with that practised North-east eye, for he replied:

'Na, na. If ye're nae in yer ain wye, ye're nae in mine.' And he carried on with what he was doing.

The journalist did not record Dr Johnson's reaction, which is a shame, for it was not often that Samuel Johnson was bettered in conversation, especially by the lower orders. We are delighted, of course, that it happened in Aberdeen.

To the best of our efforts, then, this is the first formal record of the North-east humour – and it shows very clearly the tone that has held, more or less, for more than two centuries.

We would be foolish to try to analyse humour – North-east or otherwise. We might as well try to knit treacle or juggle fog. Freud tried it and even he, the father of psychiatry, made a backside of it. So you won't find any learned or knowing analyses in this book, because only fools would try.

We can make shameless generalisations and say that the North-east humour is wry, dry and often subtle. We can say that it is at its best when cutting pomposity down to size, an age-old North-east trait. We can say that very rarely is it cruel. We can say that it is not above making fun of the North-east itself; an ability lost to too many other regions of Britain and virtually unknown in Europe.

Beyond that, we wouldn't dare insult our fellow-Neasters.

When Canongate asked us to prepare this book, both of us knew at once what sort of book we didn't want to write. Specifically, we didn't want this to be a joke book. There are plenty of joke books packing the shelves of every bookshop in Britain and covering the "humour" of almost every region of the UK. Anyone who is familiar with even a fraction of them will be struck very quickly by how similar the tales are and how most of them recycle the same basic stories and punchlines with only a change of locales and names. Shuggie in Glasgow seems to have a suspiciously similar humour to Cockney Alf, Belfast Billy and Geordie Tom. To the best of our ability, all of the tales you'll find in the next pages are verified, genuine and 100 per cent true. They actually happened, somewhere or another, all involving sons and daughters of the North-east, and the vast majority taking place in rural Aberdeenshire, Kincardine or Banffshire between World War I and the present. They have been told to us with straight faces and looks of the utmost sincerity. Those who wrote to us to share their funniest experiences or family wit generally signed off promising that we could rely on their truthfulness. So we have done. We trust them implicitly. (They were brought up in the North-east, after all.) And we're grateful to everyone who took the time and trouble to write because, without them, this book would not have been so rich a collection of North-east humour (and a lot thinner into the bargain).

Along the way, both of us have learned a very important lesson about humour of any sort. It is simply this: the best way to understand humour is not to analyse it, discuss it or pore over it. Just steep yourself in it and enjoy it.

So here are more than 250 chances to do just that.

Norman Harper and Robbie Shepherd
Aberdeen, 1996

'Stop kickin the furniture.'

Babes and Sucklings

One of the most cheering aspects of sifting through the mountains of stories was the number which proved that even primary-school children and infants are capable of the occasional blinding shaft of Doric humour. Here are a few of the best.

A MRS Yule wrote from Ellon to tell us of a neighbour, a young mum, who visited one day with her unruly son. The boy was clearly in no mood for discipline and scraped ornaments across the sideboard and threw cushions on to the floor.

'I didn't like to say anything,' wrote Mrs Yule. 'But when the boy started kicking the furniture, I coughed and glared at him. The young mother finally decided to act. "Lee!" she shouted. "Stop kickin the furniture. Ye'll spile yer new sheen."'

A THREE-YEAR-OLD from Gamrie was being corrected in his speech by his future aunt. All the best people from Gamrie are very broadly spoken, and he was certainly one of the best. At one point, he began a lively discourse on his 'moo'.

His aunt-to-be remonstrated. 'Andrew, that's your mouth, not your moo.'

He considered this for a moment. His aunt pointed to either side of his head. 'And these are your ears.'

Some time after, his grannie noticed him feeling around his head and asked if he had a problem.

'OK, Grunnie,' he said, feeling his ears, 'if this is ma ears, far's ma lugs?'

A YOUNG father on his two weeks onshore from the rigs was picking up his five-year-old son, who had just

started school at a primary not a million miles from
Turriff.

'And fit did ye learn the day?' inquired Dad.

The boy fixed him with a stare.

'That ither loons get pocket money.'

A PORTSOY mother was concerned that her eight-year-
old, David, had picked up some rather fruity language.
As mothers do, she blamed his playmates, and the other
mothers blamed David. His mother was still concerned
and asked the town bobby to have a word with her son
to see if that might scare it out of him.

One day, as David was wandering home alone from
school, the bobby spotted him, crossed the street slowly
and stopped in front of him.

'Well, David,' he said in the sternest tone he could
muster. 'I hear ye've been usin bad language.'

'Fa telt ye that?' said David.

'Oh,' said the bobby, 'a wee bird happened ontil ma
windae-sill and he telt me a' aboot it.'

'The dirty bugger,' said David. 'And efter me feedin them
ivry mornin.'

IN THE days of thatched cottages, one of the foremost
thatchers was Adam Clyne. One morning at school, the
children of one thackit hoosie were among a class being
taught the Bible.

'Now,' said the teacher, Miss McIntosh, 'does anyone
know about Adam?'

'Aye,' said one child. 'He's thackin wir hoose aenoo.'

RETIRED BANKER Edwin Reid tells of a six-year-old
who was asked what he wanted for his birthday and who
replied: 'An Autobank card.'

'An Autobank card? Fit wye?'

'Because ye get siller fanivver ye wint.'

A CHILD was asked by his primary teacher why his sister was absent from school.

'Please, miss,' said the wee lad, 'she's got a blin lump on her doup and she canna sit doon.'

'Her what?' said the teacher.

The pupil couldn't think for a wee while, then suggested: 'Please, miss, her dock.'

'Try again,' said the exasperated teacher.

The lad replied: 'Her aarse.'

In the end, admitting defeat but pointing out the error in his language, she snapped: 'Oh, sit down on your bottom,' which brought snickering around the class.

At playtime, naturally, the discussion centred on the exchange in the classroom. This brought a pensive murmur from the wee lad, who said: 'Weel, she *his* a blin lump on her erse.'

A FIRST-YEAR pupil at Fraserburgh Academy arrived late one morning for a first-period science class. When asked by the teacher for an explanation for his tardiness, he replied quite naturally: 'Sorry, miss, bit ma mither wis darnin a hole in the erse o' ma brikks.'

No sooner were the words uttered than he flushed, clapped his hands to his mouth and stuttered apologetically: 'Oh, I'm sorry, miss. I mean ma troosers.'

DURING THE war, many city people sought the relative safety of the countryside and, with a post as teacher at a nearby village, Mrs Raey rented a cottar hoose from one farming family. Young Jimmy, a boisterous four-year-old and son of the grieve at Cluny Home Farm, soon made himself acquant with daily visits, and often when the lady was in the middle of baking.

One day, he asked for a drink of milk. Mrs Raey filled the cup and handed it to the little boy, saying: 'Take care now, Jimmy; the cup is full.'

Jimmy proceeded to examine the cup, turning it round and round in his wee hands and said finally in a puzzled tone: 'It's nae fool ata, Mrs Raey. It's clean.'

ONE ASSISTANT editor with the *Press and Journal* tells of games he used to play when his two sons were small and they would try to guess what would be for tea on any given night. If their guess was wrong, he would tell them: 'Wrang spy.'

The game became a regular feature in advance of mealtimes until one day when the second boy was old enough to be asked what he would like for his tea. He thought for a few moments, then said firmly: 'I'd like some o' that Rang's Pie.'

ONE OF your co-authors has a younger brother who is still mightily embarrassed to be reminded of the day, when he was four or five, that the tyres on his tricycle went flat while he was visiting his grandfather, and he became very perplexed.

'Fit'll we dee, Ian?' asked his grandfather. 'Ye've nae air in yer tyres.'

Ian thought for a few moments, then his little face brightened. 'I ken, granda,' he said. 'We'll tak the air oot o' Norman's tyres.'

IT WAS the boy's first day at a rural school and, coming home in a foul mood, he was faced by his mother who was asking how he had got on.

'I'm nae gyaun back,' he replied firmly. 'I canna read. I canna write. And the wifie winna let me spik.'

THIS ONE is a famous North-east story and came to us in several different forms, so we have no doubt that it is true. The most common variation on the theme depicted a mother and a restless son of about four on a bus heading from Aberdeen out to Ellon. Across the gangway from them was another, younger mother and her new baby. It was obviously feeding time – judging by the continuous crying of the little one – which attracted the attention of the fidgety four-year-old.

As nature decreed, the young mum started breast-feeding the baby. The four-year-old stared in disbelief.

His mother pulled his shoulder. 'Feeding time,' she whispered. 'Now stop starin.'

'Bit mam!' he said, his eyes growing ever wider, 'he canna aet a' that athoot a tattie.'

AN ALFORD minister's wife in the 1960s used to tell of being invited to judge a children's cookery contest in the village hall and, unusually for those days, spotted a small boy as one of the contestants. He had made iced queen cakes, and when she stood in front of him she made a great show of tasting the queen cakes and saying how delicious they were. He glowed with pride.

'And tell me,' she said. 'You have such a lovely gloss on your icing. How do you manage that?'

'I lick them.'

A CONJUROR was enthralling his young audience at a Supporters' Club Children's Christmas Party at Huntly in the early 1970s. One of his tricks involved pulling eggs from a hat. As he pulled the umpteenth egg from the depths of his topper, he turned to one wee lad at the end of the front row and called: 'I bet your mother can't get eggs without hens.'

'Aye, she can,' replied the boy. 'She keeps dyeucks.'

A GAMEKEEPER at Duff House, Banff, at the turn of the century was telling his wife one night of the arrangements for the Duke of Fife's return from the Continent, and that the Duke would drive round by his lodge.

Next morning, the gamie's daugher, aged three, looked up into her mother's face and asked: 'I say, mam, will we open the gate for the dyeuck, or will he jist flee ower?'

BILL WILSON, of Peterhead, reports being on holiday in Majorca and staying at the same hotel as a young couple with two children, obviously from somewhere in the North-east.

One sunny morning, the boy, aged about six, ran to his mother. 'Mam, can I dive in the sweemin-pool?'

'No, it's ower deep for ye.'

'Bit Dad's in.'

'He's insured.'

DUNCAN FORBES, now of Elgin, tells a story from almost 30 years ago, when his five-year-old, Selina, was very quiet when she was supposed to be out the back of the house playing. Duncan fancied it was just a little too quiet and was about to go out to investigate when Selina came in through the back door.

'Fit hiv ye been deein, Selina?' asked her dad.

'Cleanin the dog's teeth,' said Selina.

'I hope ye hinna hurtit the doggie.'

'No, dad,' said Selina. 'And I'll pit back yer toothbrush, jist like I aye dee.'

A YOUNG Ellon mother was horrified when her five-year-old returned from school with his clothes torn and dirty and his face, arms and legs covered in bruises. The other boys had been throwing stones at him on the way home, he admitted.

'Well,' said his mother, 'we'd better sort this oot. Fit's their names?'

'I dinna ken their names.'

'Well, ye'd better tell yer teacher the morn. We canna pit up wi this. Bullyin needs nippin in the bud.'

'I dinna like tellin the teacher.'

'Well, if it happens again, dinna you start throwing steens back at them. You come and get me.'

'Bit you're nae eese at throwin steens.'

ONE OF your co-authors still gets mightily embarrassed when a hardy annual tale does the rounds of his family. It concerns his first school football match, when he arrived home tired, sore and dirty, but with a glow of immense satisfaction.

'And foo did ye get on?' asked his mother.

'Jist great,' he said, his little chest puffing out with pride. 'I scored a foul.'

Sweet Bird of Doric Wit

The future of any sense of humour lies in its teenagers and young adults. We're happy to report that the Doric sense of humour appears to be hale and hearty – although often unwittingly.

A PETERHEAD joiner had taken on an apprentice who was full of boundless enthusiasm, but who didn't appear to have a great deal of commonsense.

'Foo d'ye ken if ye should use a nail or a screw?' asked the joiner one morning, by way of a test.

The apprentice thought for a minute. 'Use a nail first,' he said. 'And then?' said the joiner.

'And then if the wid splits, use a screw.'

A TURRIFF lad who had had immense difficulty in finding regular work after leaving school had been signed up to the Shore Porters in Aberdeen, one of the world's oldest, most celebrated and most trusted furniture-removal firms.

When, a few weeks later, a neighbour asked his mother how Norman was getting on, she said: 'Oh, fine, fine. He's jist hid the one mischanter. He broke an expinsive Chinese pot at a hoose in Hamilton Place, and they say it wis worth near three hunder poun. So they've telt him they'll be takkin the cost oot o' his wages at three poun a wikk.'

'What rare,' said the neighbour. 'A steady job at last.'

A CLERK at a Banff law practice had struggled to make ends meet on his meagre income and finally, urged by his parents to do something about it, sought an audience with the senior partner to see if a rise wasn't in order.

The senior partner listened to the tale, but declined to offer any more money, saying that times were difficult, and so on.

'A steady job at last.'

As the dejected lad turned to go, the partner said: 'I can see you're disappointed, and I suppose you've often wondered what you would do if you had my salary, eh?'

'No,' said the lad, closing the door, 'bit I've often winnered fit ee wid dee if ee hid mine.'

AN ABERDEEN florist was waxing proud about his two children, one of whom had been accepted for Glasgow University to study medicine.

'Aye,' he said, puffing out his chest. 'I suppose ye could say – me bein a florist – that I've produced a buddin genius.'

'Aye,' muttered one nearby man to another. 'A peety the ither een's a bloomin eediot.'

ONE SMART young chap from Banchory was a student on a business-studies course at the old Robert Gordon's Institute of Technology in Aberdeen, and had been asked by the lecturer which magnate he would nominate as the world's most successful businessman.

The Deesider thought for a few moments, then said: 'Noah.'

The lecturer and all of the class were surprised, to say the least, and the lecturer demanded to know how the student had come to that conclusion.

'Well,' grinned the student. 'Noah managed to float a limited company at a time when the rest of the world was going into liquidation.'

A MR ELLIS, from Ballater, wrote to tell us of the summer he was out walking in the Deeside woods when he came upon a group of seven or eight primary-school boys flinging sticks and stones up a tree. As he drew closer, he realised their target was a red squirrel, now beside itself with fright.

'Hie!' he shouted. 'What do you think you're doing?'

The boys spun round, saw him and were decently embarrassed. It took the ringleader to explain: 'It's OK mister, we wis only tryin ti knock it doon so we could stroke it.'

ONE RECRUITING sergeant at the Aberdeen Army Careers Office tells the story of the raw North-east country lad who turned up determined to be a soldier. Despite his scrawniness and a suspicious look of being under-age, the sergeant was impressed with the lad's determination.

'How fit are you?' he boomed.

'Five fit, three inch.'

NOW THAT it is more common to see young dads pushing prams in the park, Ethel Baird, of Kincorth, tells us of seeing a young father pushing a pram round the Duthie Park in Aberdeen and mumbling something gently towards the occupant.

As he came closer to the park bench where she was feeding pigeons, she heard that he was saying: 'That's it, Darren, ye're deein fine. Jist relax. Ye're deein gran. Nae bother, Darren. It'll be OK.'

She smiled and, as they passed, congratulated him on keeping up a dialogue with his son. 'You fairly know how to speak to a baby,' she said. 'Quietly and gently.'

She stood up, leaned over the pram and said: 'And what seems to be the matter with Darren, anyway?'

'No,' said the young dad. 'He's Alan. I'm Darren.'

AN OLD farmer who didn't believe in bad weather set the men to work one absolutely foul day.

'A' them that his ileskins can gyang oot and pu neeps,' he barked.

'And fit aboot us that disna hae ileskins?' said one young lad.

'Aye,' said the farmer, 'you can dee likewise.'

THE SAME farmer was dead against smoking, and when he caught the orraloon lighting up a Woodbine up the farm close, he stopped:

'Ye can tak that thing oot o' yer face, min, and keep yer win for yer wark.'

NANCY FORSYTH wrote to tell us of her brother, Frankie, starting his apprenticeship in a garage. One day, an extremely elegant and self-important woman couldn't get her car into the garage because a lorry was parked across the entrance. She asked the lorry-driver to move the lorry, but he replied that he couldn't for a few minutes and that she would have to wait.

The woman was indignant. She puffed herself out to her full girth and snapped: 'Do you know who I am?'

The driver leaned round the side of the lorry and called to the new apprentice: 'Frunkie, awa and phone the doctor. This wifie disna ken fa she is.'

A YOUTH was lounging at a country crossroads when a man in a Riley Pathfinder stopped and asked for directions to Kinnoir. The youth never took his hands out of his pockets, but jerked his elbow in the direction of Kinnoir.

The Riley man was taken aback at the youth's slovenliness and said: 'You know, if anyone can show me a lazier trick than that, I'd be bound to give them a fiver.'

The youth, still with his hands in his pockets, stretched the pockets enough to show a space between his hands and the material and said: 'Pit it there.'

NORMAN MELDRUM, from Banff, was a champion schools debater, representing Banff Academy several times in the *Press and Journal* schools debating competition in the mid-1980s.

In 1987, he was part of the year's runner-up team, for whom the prize was a weekend's all-expenses-paid trip to

London. Part of the trip involved visiting the Greenwood Theatre for the Thursday-night taping of *Question Time*, the BBC TV discussion programme chaired then by Sir Robin Day.

Out of an audience of 300 people, it was Norman who was chosen to put the first question of the evening, on national television, to a panel of four of the country's most senior politicians, including David Owen and Joan Lestor. It was quite a task for a 16-year-old, but he carried it off with customary aplomb.

After the taping, the *Press and Journal* guests were invited into the post-recording canapés-and-wine party, attended by the production team, the political guests, a couple of Government ministers and one or two other VIPs. When Sir Robin was told that there were champion schools debaters in the assembly, he made a point of crossing the reception room to talk to them, and remembered at once that it was Norman whose question had opened the show. He congratulated him for the way he had phrased it.

'But tell me,' he said, 'I hope you weren't nervous at posing such a tough question to four of the country's most exalted notables – and on national television, too.'

'Na, na,' said Norman. 'I've been on the stage wi Robbie Shepherd.'

ONE DEESIDE builder was growing more and more frustrated with his teenage son and the lad's seeming reluctance to fix on any career. Eventually, the father decided to start him off on an apprenticeship in the building firm.

When a builder from a nearby village called in one day looking for some spare supplies, he spotted the young lad slouched in a corner of the yard, looking glumly at some two by four.

'How's the loon gettin on?' he asked.

'He's a miracle-worker,' said the father.

The visitor brightened. 'Is that so?' he said. 'Well, I'm

richt pleased ti hear it, for I kent ye werena affa sure aboot the deal ata.'

'No, he's a miracle-worker, richt enough,' said the father again. 'If ivver he dis ony work, it's a bliddy miracle.'

Kissies and Bosies

... otherwise known as Love and Marriage. North-east men are not overtly the most romantic, but deep beneath that gruff, diffident exterior beats a heart of pure mush. What woman could resist the blandishments that have worked their poetic magic and run shivers along spines down the decades, everywhere from Inverbervie to Inverallochy? Quite a few, by the sound of things.

MRS JEAN Macfarlane was a census-taker at Peterhead in 1971 before moving to Edinburgh. She recalls visiting one home in the town where a trachled-looking woman with six children aged between about two months and seven years came to the door. She was invited in and installed herself on the living-room settee.

In the course of the interview, the woman explained that her husband had died four years previously.

Mrs Macfarlane looked at the brood and wondered.

'I'm sorry,' she said. 'Maybe I misunderstood you. Did you say your husband died four years ago?'

'Aye,' said the woman then, catching the drift, added: 'He deed. I didna.'

A FRASERBURGH woman of somewhat slack reputation between the wars became the object of great interest in the community after she claimed she had been raped in the dark by a council roadman while walking home from a dance at Strichen.

'I dinna believe a word o't,' said one bustling matron to another as they queued for their groceries. 'I mean, foo did she ken it wis a roader if it wis in the dark?' 'Weel,' said the other. 'She'd likely hid ti dee a' the work.'

A NEW Pitsligo man had been discovered in flagrante with a rather attractive widow from a nearby parish. Small

The bride's mother.

villages being small villages, his wife got to hear about it and confronted him as he arrived home from work.

'There's nithing atween's,' he protested.

'Aye,' she said. 'Nae even a bliddy nichtgoon.'

A WOMAN wearing a large flowery hat arrived at a wedding at Portgordon Church in 1962 and was met by a very young and nervous usher who stopped her and asked: 'Are you a frien o' the groom?'

'No,' said the woman. 'I'm the bride's mother.'

JOHN AND Jean from Buckie had been courting for a long number of years – 30, to be exact – but there had never been a word of marriage until one day John said shyly:

'Jean, is it nae aboot time we wis thinkin o' gettin mairriet?'

'Behave yersel, John,' said Jean. 'Fa wid hae ony o' us noo?'

JIMMY HAD taken a fancy to a young lass from near Alford, but couldn't quite work out how to ask for her hand in marriage, for these were the days when fathers could still make or break a courtship.

Meg's father had a forbidding bluntness and brusqueness about him, like many farmers of his vintage, and he wasn't about to give his daughter's hand to just anyone, least of all anyone who couldn't stand up to him.

As a result, Jimmy had been slow to pluck up the courage. Little did he know it, but he had an ally in Meg's mother, who had a soft spot for him and thought that her husband had been bordering on the cruel towards the young suitor.

'I widna be surprised supposin Jimmy his a question ti ask ye, Wullie,' said Meg's mother idly one day, beginning the softening-up process.

'Oh, aye, and fit wid that be?'

'I think he's maybe hearin waddin bells.'

'Is he noo? Waddin bells? We'll see aboot that.'

'Now, Wullie. You behave yersel. And fin the time comes and he asks yer blessin, dinna you be coorse til the loon. Be nice til him.'

A few Sundays later, Jimmy turned up at an uncommon early hour before church. Meg and her mother were in the scullery.

'Is he in?' said Jimmy wanly.

'Oot the back shavin afore the Kirk,' said Meg's mother, urging him through.

Jimmy took a deep breath and shambled through to where Wullie was stooping over a basin.

'Aye-aye,' said Jimmy, by way of introduction.

Wullie looked round, then carried on shaving.

'Fine day,' said Jimmy.

'Mmphmm.'

There was an awkward pause. 'I've something ti speir at ye.'

'Oh aye.'

'A question, like.'

'Speir awa.'

'Well, I wis winderin if we could get mairriet.'

Wullie wiped the last of the soap from his face and turned to face Jimmy square on. 'Fa?' he said. 'You and me?'

A DONSIDE farmer's wife had been putting on a little more weight than was healthy and had amassed a formidable array of double chins. Still aware that her looks should be important to her, she sought a little reassurance from her husband that he still found her attractive.

'Div ye think I'm affa fat, Jock?' she inquired tentatively.

'Not a bit, quine,' he assured her.

'Is that right, Jock?' she asked, secretly delighted.

'Richt enough,' he said, turning back to his paper. 'Mind

you, there's whiles I think ye're keekin at me ower a pile o' bannocks.'

NORTH-EAST man (and woman) are not known for being very demonstrative with their public affections, but one woman was a little more forthcoming with her marital *dis*affections. Overheard at a Garioch flower show in the late 1980s, she told her companion in a stage whisper: 'Aye, the only thing ma man and me's got in common is an anniversary on the same day.'

AN OLD couple decided they would try to recapture the vigour of their courtship and romance by booking into their honeymoon hotel for the night, decades after the event.

At bedtime, Teenie was lying impatiently in the bed, waiting for Wullie, whose arthritis was making his disrobing a little slow.

'Oh, me, Wullie,' said Teenie sadly. 'I mind fan we got mairriet; ye hardly gied me time ti tak aff ma stockins. Noo I could near wyve a pair.'

A FARMER became fed up with the state his wife kept the wee bit of garden they had round the farmhouse and found himself inveigled into tidying it up. Since he felt he should be involved in the farm itself, this irked quite a bit.

One day, when the weed problem had got out of hand yet again, he decided the time had come to put his foot down.

'Na, na, na,' he stormed at his wife, 'ti hell wi this. If ye let the gairden get intil a sotter lik this again, I'll gie't a damnt gweed splash o' weedkiller.'

'A'richt,' said his wife, 'and I wid jist start pittin yer fool draaers til the cleaners.'

The Shoppie

The lifeblood of many a small village and hamlet through-out the North-east was the shoppie – fixed or mobile. Sadly, these institutions are becoming fewer and farther between, and even those that remain are losing their character and the sparkle of wit that crackled back and fore on a good day. Here are a few remembered fondly.

THE TRAVELLING fish van is still a feature of North-east life. Most come from the small fishing ports of the Moray and Banffshire coasts and ply their trade deep into the heart of Upper Banffshire, and Central and West Aberdeenshire.

One morning, at Gartly, the fishman bowled up at one of his regular customers, who appeared with a stranger at her side. This turned out to be a visitor from Aberdeen, and rather a plummy visitor, at that.

When the lady of the house had received her usual order, the fishman turned his attention to the visitor. 'And fit aboot you, ma dear?' he inquired.

'Is your fish really fresh?' she said haughtily.

'Really fresh?' he said. 'Look at them!'

Then he turned to the fillets, lying there on a tin tray, and slapped two or three.

'For God's sake!' he shouted at them. 'I've telt ye afore! Can ye nae lie still!'

SIGNS in a shop near New Deer. The outside of the door bears the legend:

N S Y

The inside of the same door reads:

S Y OOT

TINKER FAMILIES plied North-east doors for trade as late as the early 1970s, and one squad was out near Keith

'Can ye nae lie still!'

trying to get rid of as many carpet offcuts and, frankly, moth-eaten fireside rugs as they could. When they stopped at one abode in Moss Street, the lady of the house was having none of it.

'Certainly not,' she said imperiously. 'Michty, yer carpets is stinkin.'

'That's nae the carpets, wifie,' said the tinker. 'That's me.'

ADAM REID was a tailor in Alford. One day in the early 1950s, he told a prominent farmer and church elder who had been fitted for a suit that the suit would be ready in six weeks.

'Sax wikks?' said the farmer. 'That's nae eese ti me; I need it for a waddin in a fortnicht. Michty, it jist took the Lord sax days ti mak the warld.'

'Aye,' said Adam, unimpressed. 'And look at fit a sotter it's in.'

BILL DONALD ran a shop selling, installing and servicing TVs. One day, in the mid-1960s, he took a call from a woman at Glenkindie who was complaining about the quality of her picture.

'Fit exactly's wrang wi yer picter?' he inquired.

'Weel,' said the woman, 'I've the news on aenoo and the blokie readin the news his got an affa lang face.'

'Aye,' said Bill, 'if I wis readin the news nooadays, I wid hae a lang face, tee.'

A BETTERWEAR salesman who had taken a job in the Inverurie area in the 1970s – and is now a prominent Aberdeen businessman – was out in the Garioch trying to drum up trade when he went up to a cottar hoose and knocked sharply. A small boy came to the door.

'Hullo, ma wee lad. Is your mummy in?'

The boy shook his head.

'Is your daddy in?'

The boy shook his head again.

'Well, is there anyone else in that I could speak to?'

The small boy nodded and said. 'Ma sister.'

'OK, can I speak to her?'

So the small boy trotted back into the house and was gone for fully five minutes. Then the boy returned alone and said: 'I canna lift her oot o' the playpen.'

A SHOPKEEPER at Banff who happened also to be a prominent after-dinner speaker along the Moray Firth coast remembers being overcome at a football-club dinner at Fraserburgh and falling back into his seat. A large crowd gathered round about him and, in his daze, he remembers hearing them clamouring: 'Move back! Move back!'

He also remembers the wife of one of the club officials shouting: 'Gie him some whisky! Gie him some whisky!'

Others began shouting: 'He needs air! He needs air!'

But still the woman insisted: 'Gie him some whisky! Gie him some whisky!'

Up went shouts of: 'Get an ambulance! Get an ambulance!'

And still the woman insisted: 'Gie him some whisky! Gie him some whisky!'

'Eventually,' he said, 'I raised my head and said: "For ony sake, will somebody listen til the wumman?"'

AN ABERDONIAN who had been imprisoned in Singapore during the war returned to the Granite City after being repatriated and decided that the first thing he wanted to do was to buy himself the bottle of whisky he had dreamed about for so many years in captivity.

At that time, whisky was still in short supply and could be sold only in licensed grocers and pubs within stated licensing hours. A man who had been a prisoner of the Japanese for so many years was a little out of touch with the new customs and went into a back-street Aberdeen grocer who had one bottle of whisky on display in his window.

The PoW went in and said that he wanted to buy the bottle.

'Ye canna buy it,' said the young man, mindful of the licensing laws. 'It's nae 'oors.'

'Well,' said the mystified PoW, 'if it's not yours, why have you got it in your window?'

MAGGIE AND Bessie were two sisters, both now deceased, who were among the most colourful characters in the Howe of Alford. Having been invited to a wedding, Bessie made a rare visit to the hairdresser and announced that she wanted 'the works'.

Worried that an old lady might be alarmed at having to lean backwards over the sink to have her hair washed, the hairdresser asked thoughtfully: 'Wid ye like the back wash for yer hair, Bessie?'

Bessie glared at her.

'The back wash? I'm needin the hale lot washed!'

MAD COW Disease has frightened too many North-east butchery customers for the liking of the trade or of beef farmers, most of whom blame the media for blowing a problem into an epidemic.

One well-known Inverurie lady visited one of the town butchers early in 1993 and was greeted by the usual cheery voice from behind the counter.

'Weel, Mrs Mc——, fit'll it be the day? The usual bit silverside for yer broth?'

'Damn the linth wi yer silverside,' snapped the customer. 'I've heard a' aboot this Mad Coo Disease. Keep yer silverside. I'll hae a pun o' mince.'

THE SAME butcher reports his experience with a very difficult customer, known with shopkeepers throughout the town for finding fault with everything. There wasn't a please in her.

The butcher had employed a new apprentice and was interested to see how the young lad would cope with Mrs Difficult. He gave the lad no warning when, as usual, she turned up for her Thursday morning bit of brisket and a hen for the broth.

'Hmm,' she said, peering at the chicken the lad had offered her. 'That disna look affa fresh. It's a bit scrawny. Hiv ye nae nithing better?'

The lad said that that was the last hen they had in stock until later that day. Mrs Difficult asked to see the hen again, and peered at it all the harder, from every angle.

'Ye can see fit I mean, I'm sure,' she said. 'Its skin's a' slack and there's nae muckle meat on it.' She leaned a bit closer and sniffed. 'And I'm nae sure bit fit it's on the turn.'

The butcher says he could hardly control his pleasure when the lad said: 'And could ye stand the same inspection yersel?'

A CULLEN fisher couldn't get rid of a sore throat, so his wife went down to Balfour the Chemist for some pastilles or similar soothers. The chemist recommended a particular brand and gave the wife instructions to dissolve one tablet in the mouth as required.

She was back at the chemist within the hour.

'Excuse me, cheemist,' she said, 'dis he swalla the bree?'

JOHN MUSTARD had the souter's shop (shoemaker) at Cullen a few years back and was working away in his back shop one day when he was surprised to see at the counter a young lad asking if he could come and see his father in a hurry.

John knew of the family, but he was not well-acquainted

with them. Whatever, he decided he had better do as he had been bidden and see what the problem was. He left his brother in charge of the shop and set off with the wee lad.

It was a wasted journey. The boy had been following instructions from his father, who had been about to sit down to his tea and had told his son: 'Awa and get me mustard.'

AN ABERCHIRDER shop assistant was heard discussing how hard it was to get by on a shop assistant's salary and was drawing much sympathy and empathy from one elderly customer, who said: 'I ken fit it's like. In my young day, I'd an affa job makkin ends meet.'

'I'm nae sae much worriet aboot makkin the ends meet,' said the girl, 'though it wid be real fine if they could get close enough ti wave at een anither noo and again.'

LONG BEFORE the days when we all became so sophisticated, and we all believed in the healing powers of the weird and wonderful cures hawked round the doors by quack doctors, one tinker was plying his trade round homes at Stonehaven, trying to sell bottles of so-called hair-restorer.

Ethel Baird, now of Kincorth, wrote to tell us that her mother had gone to the door to be confronted with the salesman and was not slow to point out that if his hair restorer was so marvellous, why did he not use some of it himself, for he was as bald as a ladle. 'It's a funny salesman that doesn't use his own product.'

Without dallying, the tinker replied: 'Aye, but why should I? Hugh Ramsay (the town draper) sells corsets.'

Down on the Farm

Although you would never think so to listen to them, some of the best of North-east humour comes from farming circles, particularly once the farmers get together socially, and any non-farmer who manages to inveigle himself into their company is assured an entertaining few hours.

AT A DINNER held by the National Farmers' Union in Aberdeen, and attended by some of the wealthiest tillers of the soil the North-east of Scotland can boast, the guests were not greatly impressed by the after-dinner speaker – a dull, wordy and not particularly entertaining councillor.

A Huntly farmer leaned to the man on his right and said: 'I've nivver really heard an efter-dinner speech worth listenin til. Hiv you?'

'Michty aye,' said the other. 'Last wikk, I wis oot wi the bunker and he said: "I'll pey the bill."'

A VET near Inverurie had been attending the very difficult birth of a calf. The labour had taken most of the night and everyone in attendance – vet, farmer, wife and son – was exhausted.

Finally, at six in the morning, just as the farmer's youngest son, aged seven, appeared in the doorway, the calf fell on to the straw to a great cacophony of mooing from the proud mother, and sighs of relief and tiredness from the four humans.

The farmer's eldest son, leaning on a byre post, exhausted, said: 'Fit is't?' – meaning was the newborn male or female, for in all the excitement they had been too busy to take note.

The small boy who had just appeared was standing by and said shyly: 'Gies a look at the calfie. I ken foo ye can tell.'

A FARM labourer convicted of lewd behaviour involving a cow had been fined at Banff Sheriff Court and – somewhat unwisely, it must be said – had decided to visit a café in the town for his lunch before returning to the farm.

Without a word, a waitress appeared and laid in front of him a plate of carrot tops, oatmeal, grass and dockens.

He stared at the plate and looked up at her, incredulous. 'Fit's this?' he demanded. 'I canna aet this.'

'No?' she said. 'Well, if you canna, jist gie it til yer girlfriend.'

A FARMER had been refused planning permission for a new house for his son, and so had to resort to finding a cottage somewhere near Rothienorman. He had inquired with all the nearby farmers to see if they had anything spare that they might sell, but none had.

Eventually, he took his son to see an estate agent at Inverurie, but everything on the agent's books was either too far away, too big or, more often, too expensive.

By the time they came to the last property on file, the farmer took off his bunnet, sighed, and ran a hand through his hair. 'Lord,' he said. 'Hiv ye nithing for aboot twa thoosan?'

'I'm sure,' said the estate agent. 'Come oot wi me the morn's mornin and we'll see if it's still stannin.'

A PROMINENT farming family in Aberdeenshire (whom we won't name because they are still in situ) were mildly resented in the nearby community for the way they spent their money in what the townsfolk judged was the flashiest way possible. The family's children, according to local opinion, were indulged right from birth to the time each made its own way in the world.

When the business venture of one collapsed, it became the speak of the place, particularly at the mart, where one farmer observed drily: 'Life hisna been easy for young ——.

The girlfriend's special

He'll ken aboot problems noo that it's a' collapsed roon aboot his heid.'

'Aye,' said the other. 'Problems, richt enough. I doot he'll jist hae ti grit his teeth, roll up his sleeves and ask his faither for anither fifty thoosan.'

THE GREAT drought of 1976 reduced virtually all the North-east farming population to despair, to such a degree that one Ellon minister prayed from the pulpit for rain. On the Monday, one of the most violent thunderstorms in years drenched the area and ruined a large acreage of what crops existed.

'And that's the trouble wi the meenister,' one farmer announced to another at the mart later that week. 'He aye overdis things.'

A FORMER lecturer at the North of Scotland College of Agriculture in Aberdeen swears that this story, from the early 1960s, is true. A chicken farmer near Laurencekirk was losing a lot of his stock, despite the intervention of vets, and decided as a last resort to write to the college to see if they had any advice.

'Every morning, when I go out, I find two or three more lying on the ground, cold and stiff, with their legs in the air. Can you tell me what is the matter?'

A few days later, he received a reply: 'Dear Mr ——. Your hens are dead.'

A FORMER waitress at the Northern Hotel, Kittybrewster, Aberdeen, wrote to us and sought anonymity for her tale from the days when the biggest mart in the North of Scotland was held every Friday just a few hundred yards along the road from the hotel, and farmers from five counties and beyond converged to do business or just have a news.

One particular Strathbogie farmer was a notorious twister, who was never slow to try to get something for nothing.

Our waitress recalled him turning up and asking for a plate of mince and tatties. This was duly served him but, before he started tucking in, he asked if he could change his mind and have a plate of the steak-and-kidney pie, instead. The waitress obliged; removed the mince and tatties, and returned five minutes later with the pie, which he ate hungrily.

He stood up and was walking out when the waitress caught him near the front door and reminded him that he hadn't paid.

'Aye, aye, lassie, bit if I mind richt I gied ye a plate o' mince and tatties for the steak-and-kidney pie, did I nae?'

'Well, yes, but you didn't pay for the mince and tatties.'

'Bit I didna aet the mince and tatties, so fit wye should I pey for it?'

THE DRAM after paying the hairst bill is a custom throughout the North-east, and probably far beyond. One farmer's wife from near Oyne told us of the evening in the late 1970s when the combine-owner had called to seek his due and her man had reached for the bottle of Grouse to seal the deal.

Both men sat down, but the visitor was looking into the dram very glumly.

'Is there something adee?' inquired the farmer.

'There's a flee in ma dram, min,' said the visitor.

'Oh, I'm sorry aboot that,' said the farmer's wife, stepping in to retrieve the glass.

'Na, na,' said the visitor, pulling the glass back closer to himself. 'I'm nae bothered aboot the flee – jist the wye it's widin across the boddim.'

A CROFTER from Craigievar paid an evening visit to a

neighbouring farm. The crofter had spent most of his life as a cattleman on various farms, breeding Aberdeen-Angus and Shorthorn cattle.

On being asked into the farmhouse for a fly cup, the conversation between the two men inevitably was of pedigree cattle.

After a considerable time, the farmer's wife felt the need to change the subject of the conversation and tried to steer it round by asking the crofter how his niece was getting on now that she had gone to Aberdeen to work.

'Deein gran,' said the crofter. 'She's got a job as a shorthorn-typist.'

TWO CROFTER brothers were drying off at the fireside in their wee hoose after a pouring wet day in the fields.

'I winder if the rain's stoppit yet,' said one.

'Dinna ken,' said the other. 'I hinna been oot since I come in.'

IN THE 1990s, it is known as 'an insurance job', but several decades ago no one could be so openly suspicious of a neighbour or friend, least of all in the farming community, but there were ways and ways.

A fire broke out in one Buchan farmer's strae-ricks early one morning, and a troupe of neighbours turned out to do what they could to douse the flames, but to little effect.

The farmer stepped away, looking extremely calm, took out his pipe and lit his tobacco. One of his exhausted neighbours turned to him.

'Weel, weel, Geordie,' he said. 'I doot that's nae the first time yer spunks hiv been oot the day.'

WE HAD better keep the names here secret, but the story involves a farmer near Dunecht, whose farm was being inspected by a representative of the Ministry of Agriculture.

Being invited into the farmhouse, the ministry man said he would be delighted to meet Mrs G——.

'Aweel,' said the farmer, 'come awa in. I hinna a bonnie wife, bit I can show ye some real bonnie coos.'

JUST BEFORE the end of World War I, a group of Garioch farmers were at the mart discussing what punishment would be suitable for the Kaiser for all the havoc, death and destruction he and his like had wrought.

Many punishments were dreamed up, each more vicious than the one before, but they fixed on what they thought was the best of the lot.

They would give him an overdraft on a small, north-facing croft at Rhynie.

WE DEBATED long and hard over whether or not to include this one at all, for it is easily the least tasteful story in the book, but on the grounds that North-east people are not easily shockable, it is included. We won't embarrass the contributor by naming him. If you are easily shockable yourself, close your eyes now.

A Peterhead farmer went into the chemist in 1962 for a packet of condoms, 'Foo muckle's that?' he inquired.

'One pound, plus tax,' said the assistant.

'Nivver mind the tacks,' he said. 'I'll jist tie them on wi binder twine.'

THE DAYS of the travelling threshing-mill round the crofts showed North-east community spirit at its best, with neighbour helping neighbour. At dinnertime or teatime, the small living room of the croft being hairstit would be full to overflowing.

Always, two men would arrive the night before with the steam mill so that they could set it up in fine time for an early yokin the following morning.

At this particular croft, the two steam-mill men were not

known to the crofter's wife, but she was mindful of her duty in making sure that they felt welcome when they arrived for their meal.

'Aet up stem-mull man,' she said. 'Aet up at man aside ye.'

IT HAD been a particularly boring football match at Pittodrie. The Dons certainly had not been at their best, and the final whistle blew with the scoresheet blank.

A group of Kemnay farm workers was making a slow, dejected exit, when one looked at another and said: 'We'd hiv been as weel at hame githerin steens.'

IT HAD been a most enjoyable day at the sheepdog trials at Monymusk. The competitions were over and the post-mortems had to be conducted over a sociable dram. This meant that Dod stayed longer than he had intended, and all thoughts of the raging wife at home had long since evaporated.

It wasn't until he was dropped off at the end of the road that he began to panic. We didn't discover what happened next until the following sheepdog trial when Dod, fortified with the barley bree again, explained.

His wife, apparently, had gone to bed already by the time he had got home. He crept upstairs as slowly and as quietly as his delicate state would allow. He had just reached the top of the stairs and had pushed open the door gently when his wife stirred.

'I jist crawlt in on all fours til the bedside,' said Dod, 'and the wife pit oot her haun, sayin: "Is that you, Flossie?"'

'Did ye get aff wi't, Dod?' inquired a crony.

'I did,' said Dod. 'I hid the presence o' mind ti lick her haun.'

TWO Oldmeldrum farmers had met at the local smiddy in the late 1950s. One was known to be very young, thrusting and ambitious, with an eye to maximum productivity and new methods. The other was of the old school.

Passing the time of day while the smith attended to their needs, the younger was heard to remark that he was planning to erect a massing building on his land. It would be hundreds of yards long and hundreds of yards wide and a good few yards in height. It would be one of the grandest buildings in the Garioch. And what scope it would give him once it was finished.

After he had finished telling of his plans, he waited for the older farmer to be suitably admiring, but the reply was:

'Aye, aye, aye. Bit far I come fae we like ti ploo a bit o' the grun, an a'.'

MANY YEARS ago, there was a particularly impressive bull at Tarland, which gave the farmer immense pride and, in truth, caused a lot of admiration around the Howe of Cromar. One day, the minister called and asked if he might see this bull that everyone was talking about and the farmer agreed readily and began walking towards a nearby field.

'Oh,' said the minister, 'I had assumed it would be safely locked up in a stall, where I could see it at close quarters.'

'Na, na, meenister,' said the farmer. 'It's oot in the park.'

The minister followed, a little more reluctantly, and soon saw the massive animal, standing alone in the centre of a field. He swallowed a little.

The farmer stopped beside the gate and bade the minister jump in over. The minister clambered in over with a little difficulty and waited for the farmer to join him. But the farmer stayed where he was, leaning on the outside of the gate.

'Are you not coming, too?' inquired the minister.

'Na, na,' said the farmer. 'I ken fit he looks like. I've seen him plenty o' times. Awa ye go.'

The minister thought for a moment, summoned his courage and began stepping gingerly towards the centre of the park. Half-way, he stopped, turned and said: 'What if he charges?'

'He winna charge,' said the farmer. 'Ye dinna think I'd pit ye in there yersel if he wis the kinna bull that charged.'

'No, but just supposing he does charge. What do I do?'

'Weel,' said the farmer. 'I wid turn roon, pick up a handfae and fling it at him.'

'A handful of what?'

'Dinna worry,' said the farmer. 'It'll be there.'

Characters

Every city and region has its characters, and Aberdeen and the North-east would appear to have more than their fair share.

BERT DUNCAN, from Woodside, Aberdeen, became celebrated in the shadowy world of London boxing as one of the finest corners a boxer could hope to have supporting him. During one fight, in the mid-1950s, Bert was accompanying a distinctly unimpressive boxer from the dressing-room to the ring.

'It's a long way, isn't it?' said the boxer.

'Dinna worry,' growled Bert. 'Ye winna be walkin back.'

ONE OF the North-east's most celebrated auctioneers is Bill Lippe, whose evenings at Kemnay draw crowds for miles. One evening, the story goes, a handsome stuffed parrot in a large cage appeared. Bidding for Lot 165 began at £10. Bill was surprised that interest took off quite as spectacularly as it did – and certainly far in excess of what he judged the lot was worth.

Finally, just two bidders were in competition with one another: a farmer's wife from Blairdaff and an unknown voice across at the front, right-hand corner of the village hall.

People round about the Blairdaff woman were growing gradually more incredulous that she should be thinking of spending such money on a stuffed parrot, but she had a determined set about her jaw and was clearly intent on winning.

Finally, at £85, the prize was hers and two farmers nearby leaned across to congratulate her. 'Well, Mrs——,' said one. 'At that price, I hope he's a good spikker.'

'Och, he's a rare spikker,' said the other. 'Fa div ye think she wis biddin against?'

PAT BUCHAN, who used to teach dancing around Edinburgh before retiring back to his native Peterhead in the mid-1950s, used to tell of teaching a class of novices at a well-known school for the well-heeled young lady and taking, as a partner, a very nervous and easily embarrassed young deb.

He instructed her to watch his feet carefully and to try to follow everything he did.

She was so desperate to do well that she kept one step ahead of him all the time, without waiting for his lead. After several stops and starts, he admitted to growing a little impatient and eventually stopped, sighed and said: 'I'm sorry, but yer problem is that ye're anticipatin.'

'I am not!' she blushed. 'I'm not even married!'

WILLIE LUMSDEN was a passenger porter at Inverurie Railway Station for almost half a century, a well-kent figure and known to almost everyone who travelled on the line, and certainly to every soul in the Garioch.

He also dabbled as an amateur chiropodist, in days when farmers and farmworkers suffered all manner of problems because their feet were expected to withstand the harshest of winters, the poorest of footwear and the most neglectful of care.

One evening, an unnamed farmworker turned up to have a particularly ugly foot attended to. Willie did the best he could and the client put his sock and boot back on again.

'Oh, what fine, Wullie,' he said, sighing with pleasure. 'I wish noo that I'd washed ma ither fit.'

MAGGIE, A waitress at the former Gloucester Hotel in Union Street, Aberdeen, reports working for one summer season with a country-bred waitress who stood no nonsense from anyone.

When one diner complained that he had detected no hint of oxtail in the oxtail soup, she glared at him, snatched

One step ahead

the plate and announced: 'And ye'll be disappintit ti hear there's nae horse in wir horseradish, eether.'

MAGGIE'S COLLEAGUE had been asked to stand in for an afternoon behind reception to cover for a receptionist who had become ill. When one guest approached to ask if he could buy stamps for a parcel, Maggie's colleague raked about among the drawers and found a sheet of stamps.

She tore off the requisite amount and the man pushed the right number of coins across the counter, as well as the parcel. Maggie's colleague's stare told the man that she was not prepared to do anything more for him.

'W-well,' he said, hesitating. 'Will I stick the stamps on myself?'

'Please yersel,' said Maggie's colleague. 'Though ye'd likely be better stickin them on yer parcel.'

THE SAME lady was back in the dining-room and had been confronted by a QC up from Edinburgh who was having a quick lunch during recess from court and who was clearly not impressed with the cuisine and called her over to say so.

'I have a complaint,' he said.

'This is a hotel,' she said, cruising past. 'Nae a hospital.'

IT WAS the night of the Harvest Home dance at the big hoose, when the laird and his entourage mixed with tenants, estate workers, guests and villagers to celebrate the end of the harvest.

In the middle of an eightsome reel, the second horseman, fortified with the dram, engaged the laird in conversation.

'Man, fit a gran nicht. I'm fair conspirin.'

'Conspiring?' queried his lordship. 'Conspiring means "to plot".'

''At's richt, min,' said the horseman. 'I'm fair plottin.'

JOHN DUNCAN, of Dubbieford Farm, near Torphins, enjoyed long and strong friendships in the community and was highly regarded by all who knew him. Jack Kellas, of Torphins, wrote to tell us of a bit news he had once with Dubbie when the subject worked its way round to fenceposts.

Jack offered Dubbie the chance to buy some surplus that he happened to have after buying more than he found he needed.

'Fit like a price wid ye be needin?' inquired Dubbie.

'Twa shillins apiece,' said Jack. 'They're oak. They'll laist for ivver.'

Dubbie rubbed his chin. 'Ah, bit ye're gey strong in the price, Jake. Dam't, ye're needin ower muckle, I'm thinkin.'

Jack thought for a moment. 'Well, fit aboot a shillin each? A real bargain.'

'Weel, ye are saftenin a bittie bit, ach, ye ken, I'm nae sair-needin posts aenoo. Ma fences is real snod.'

'Right, John,' said Jack, 'I'll tell ye fit: ye can hae the twinty posts for nithing. Will that please ye?'

Dubbie grasped him by the shoulder, grinning. 'Now, haud on Jake, haud on,' he said. 'Is that delivered?'

JACK KELLAS tells also of another good neighbour, farmer George Anderson, who was summoned to attend the Inland Revenue office in Aberdeen for an investigation of his accounts. George was reluctant to go, but was persuaded that it would be better in the long run to get the matter cleared up. Not every farmer in those days had a car, but a neighbouring farmer, Hilly, offered to run him into town.

The two set off on Friday morning and, after attending the mart at Kittybrewster, made their way down town to the Inland Revenue office. On arrival, Hilly suggested that he would sit outside in the car while George set about his business with the tax man.

'Na, na,' insisted George. 'Ye're nae sittin oot here stairvin. Ye'd better come awa in and see fit this bliddy mannie his ti say.'

Once the tax inspector was persuaded that it would be all right for a third party to be present while Mr Anderson's accounts were examined, they set about taking the books through hand.

'Now, Mr Anderson,' said the inspector, poring over sheets of figures. 'I see that at the start of your year you had six hundred head of poultry. Is that correct?'

'Michty aye.'

'And you bought four hundred and fifty during the year?'

'Aye.'

'Well, there is something far wrong here, it seems to me. You have no sales recorded during the year and your closing valuation number is only seven hundred. What happened to the other three hundred and fifty? Do you still have them?'

'No,' said Geordie, becoming a little uncomfortable. 'I hinna.'

'You don't have them?'

'No.'

'So where do you suppose they might be then?'

'I suppose they must hiv dee't.'

'Died? Three hundred and fifty of your poultry have died? What on earth could they have died of?'

Geordie fixed him with a stare.

'The skitter.'

WE'D BETTER not reveal the man's name, but we'll call him Jock the Coalman. A week before Christmas a few years back, the conversation in the village pub got round to finding a bird for the Christmas Day table, and memories of the size of some turkeys they had seen over the years.

Jock listened in silence as one of the worthies continually topped everyone else's stories with a 30-pounder he'd had a few years previously.

'And fit aboot yersel, Jock?' somebody asked. 'Fit's the biggest turkey ee've ivver seen?'

'Weel,' drawled Jock, 'fin I come awa fae the hoose this mornin, the wife wis dressin oor turkey, and it wis that big she wis rowin stuffin up its erse wi a box barra.'

BRYAN SMITH, now of Aberdeen, tells a story from his wartime days in the Far East, much adapted by after-dinner speakers ever since, but this is the original.

It concerns Waddy, third horseman at Drumdelgie, and then in the 9th Battalion Gordon Highlanders. In January, 1945, they were crossing the Irrawaddy when they were divebombed by six Japanese Zero fighters. Mr Smith's batman was shot through the head. Waddy received a leg wound and was removed to a forward casualty-clearing station behind the lines.

Who should appear shortly afterwards but Field Marshal Sir Bill Slim. The great man spotted Waddy, lying there, smoking the ubiquitous stubby pipe so beloved of farm servants between the wars, and wreathed in clouds of XX Bogie Roll. The field marshal bent down and inquired of Waddy: 'Tell me, man, where exactly were you wounded?'

Waddy pondered for a moment, sat up and replied: 'Weel, sir, I jaloose it wid hiv been a twa-three mile the Huntly side o' the Irrawaddy.'

THE LATE Jock Strachan was a well-known and well-respected farmer in the Fyvie area. One evening, he turned up at a concert at Fyvie and the compere of the show noticed that Jock was present. Between two of the acts, the compere told the story of a teacher asking her class for definitions of words, and she had asked for a definition of the word Nothing.

A boy had shot up his hand and had said: 'Please, miss, it's fit ye get for haudin Jock Strachan's horse.'

ONE EVENING, a group of Oldmeldrum worthies were discussing the forthcoming Oldmeldrum Sports, that annual gala which is as much a part of North-east culture as the Turriff Show, the Lonach or the Braemar Gathering.

'Ach, I'm nae gyaun this eer,' said Jock. 'It's aye the same. Quines duncin. Bill Anderson throwin his haimmer farrer than the neist lad. Tugga-war. Pipers dirlin a'b'dy's lugs. Nithing new. Na na, nae for me.'

'Oh, bit ye're wrang,' said Sandy. 'For instance, tak the pageant. This year, the theme's Legends Throweoot The Centuries, and I hear say that the Meldrum Rural wifies are gaun as Lady Godiva – ye ken, the wifie that rode throwe the streets bare-nakit, tirred til the skin o' a fite horse.'

'Ach,' said Jock, 'maybe I will ging. It's a filie sin I've seen a fite horse.'

WILLIE WEBSTER was the joiner at Methlick and, in the 1950s, was visited by the factory inspector who demanded to see the joinery's fire extinguisher.

'Up in the laft,' said Willie.

The inspector was perplexed, for he could see no stair to the loft. 'Mr Webster, how do I get up there?'

'Use a laidder.'

Willie produced a ladder and the inspector proceeded, shakily, into the loft, where he found the extinguisher under a pile of old sacks – hardly the most accessible point in case of emergency.

But, worse, it was empty.

'Of coorse it's impty,' snapped Willie. 'If I kept it full, it wid jist roost.'

'And what would you do if there was a fire?'
'Fill it, of coorse.'

AT INSCH Station, one gate of the level crossing was shut, but the other was left open. Peter Scatterty, on duty as signalman, was asked by Harry Usher what was going on.

'Well,' said Peter. 'I'm half-expectin a train.'

AT A major Fiddlers' Spectacular at HM Theatre, Aberdeen, there was an age gap of 85 years between the youngest and the oldest of the 100 assembled musicians – the youngest was nine and the oldest, Harry Nicol, of Cults, a mere 94.

After a day-long dress rehearsal before the week's show, Harry went into his local at the Ploughman, Culter, for a wee dram to ease away the other elbow exertions on the stage. His trusty fiddle was in its case under his arm as he made his way to the bar. The proprietor greeted him with: 'Michty, Harry, far hiv ye been?'

'I've been awa for a practice,' said Harry.

'Michty,' said mine host, 'at your age, min, if ye canna play the damnt thing afore this time, it's hardly worth yer file yokin.'

IN THE mid-1960s, BBC Scotland staged a grand fiddle concert at Blair Castle, home of the Duke of Atholl. The concert featured fiddlers from throughout Scotland and producer James Hunter had persuaded noted virtuoso Yehudi Menuhin to take part. Menuhin was, and still is, most appreciative of the Scottish style of fiddle-playing, but expressed reservations on being able to handle the technique at short notice.

Some of the fiddlers on stage, to put it mildly, were more enthusiastic than expert, and so it was at rehearsal

that the guest was shown a seat between two elderly
fiddlers of rural stock, who fitted in well in strathspey-
and-reel circles, but never professed to being individ-
ual stars.

'Gentlemen,' said Menuhin, 'thanks for the honour, but
I must confess to being a little apprehensive and nervous
in following your music.'

'Nivver ee mind, chiel,' said the lad on his right. 'Ye're
atween twa gweed men.'

NO TRUE man or woman of the North-east has not
heard of Jamie Fleeman. The Laird O' Udny's Feel, as
he was known, was born in 1723 and spent most of his
working life as manservant to the Laird of Udny Castle
in Aberdeenshire. He was of simple mind, but his loyalty
to the laird was staunch, although he often despised the
laird's friends, perhaps because they thought they could get
away with poking sarcastic jibes at 'the fool', but it was
Jamie who always got the better of them, and the stories
are legend.

One of the landed gentry had been a guest of Udny and
had made some remark that had upset Jamie. Revenge came
the next morning as Jamie was having a wee snooze on the
banks of the Ythan when the guest appeared at the other
side of the river with his horse.

He shouted across and asked Jamie where the best
crossing-point would be. Jamie directed him to the deep-
est bit of the water. The gentleman urged his horse in
and both promptly disappeared. The gentleman nearly
drowned.

Spitting with rage, and utterly drenched, he hauled
himself back out on to the bank and shouted that Jamie
had tried to kill him.

'Gweed be here,' cried Jamie, 'I've seen the geese and
the dyeucks crossin there hunders o' times, and surely yer
horse his langer legs nor them.'

THEN THERE was the time Jamie was staying at another house and the proprietor and his factor were nearby, discussing a poor crop.

'I've tried many things,' said the factor, 'but nothing seems to grow.'

The man of business, with scant knowledge of farming, mused for a time and was about to give his considered opinion when Jamie interjected, counting factors well down his list of useful articles.

'I cwid tell ye fit wid thrive in't. Plunt it wi factors. They thrive onywye.'

JAMIE, OF course, got his by-name of The Laird o' Udny's Fool when he met one of the laird's titled friends in the grounds of the castle.

'Who are you?' asked the gentleman with a superior air.

'I'm the Laird o' Udny's feel,' said Jamie. 'Fa's feel are ee?'

REUBEN RAE was a character well known around Kintore in the 1920s, and there was nothing he liked better than to get a lot of young lads round about him so he could boast of all his achievements. The lads were in awe of him, swearing that he was surely in league with the devil.

One of Reuben's tales was of the time a Kintore farmer sent for him as the farm was over-run with rabbits. The farmer met the newly employed trapper a few days later and asked how he was getting on.

'Weel,' Reuben replied, 'last nicht I set thirty-sax snares, and this mornin I hid thirty-sax rubbits and twa wytin ti get in.'

ANOTHER KINTORE worthy was Jamie Will. One day, the young lads had congregated round the fountain when Jamie came past aboard his rather ancient wreck of a bicycle. It was rumoured that he was courting a lass at Balmoral and was en route.

One of the lads suggested: 'It'll tak ye a gey file on that bike, Jamie.'

'Na na,' replied Jamie, sailing past, 'this is ma Sunday bike. Nineteen gears, and fin I get into tap gear, ilky crunk's a quarter o' a mile.'

WILLIE LOW, of Glassel, was a well-known dealer, and plenty of stories are attributed to him. Willie had sold a heifer to a neighbouring farmer for £440. Unfortunately, the heifer died a week later, so back came the purchaser to complain and seek recompense.

'Man, Wullie, this is nae damnt eese,' stormed the farmer.

'Fit's adee?' said Willie.

'The heifer's dee't.'

'Man,' said Willie. 'It nivver did that fin I hid it.'

THE INTERNATIONALLY known firm of R.B. Farquhar Ltd. was founded by Rab Farquhar, of Rhynie, who started out his business life selling firewood round doors. He never lost the common touch as he became a millionaire, flying the globe to do oil-industry deals. To his immense credit, neither did he lose his strong North-east accent and ways.

Retired banker Edwin Reid had introduced Rab to a British government minister after the minister had made an important speech at the Whitehall Hotel, Houston, Texas.

'Pleased to meet you Mr Farkwar,' said the minister, 'and what do you do for a living?'

Rab didn't like being referred to as Farkwar, but he replied: 'Oh, I jist mak things beginnin wi S.'

'Things beginning with S?' said the minister. 'What sort of things beginning with S?'

'Oh,' said Rab, 'sheds, chalets and shitehooses.'

ON ANOTHER visit to Houston, Edwin took Rab up a

downtown skyscraper to view the big city and Mr F. was duly impressed. On their way out, the commissionaire said to the pair of them: 'Y'all have a good weekend, hear?'

Bob turned to Edwin and remarked: 'It was affa nice o' that chiel ti say that we maun hae a nice wikkenn,' so Edwin suggested that when Rab got home he should stand at the gates of his factory and greet all his workers with: 'Have a pleasant weekend.'

'Na, na, na,' said Rab. 'I couldna dee that. They wid say that Farquhar's aff his heid.'

RAB BUILT and owned a chalet holiday complex at Callander, and would make frequent runs down in his Rolls-Royce to check up on standards and to be sure that everything was in order. One day when he arrived, he found that the handyman was missing, so he went into the shed, put on a pair of dungarees and started up the mower.

The sound of the mower brought out the slumbering holidaymakers, who were delighted to see a member of staff so that they could bring to his attention whatever little problems they had encountered, from blown light bulbs to new supplies of toilet paper.

Rab delighted in finishing this tale with: 'Ye ken this. I workit real hard aa day and finished up wi a fiver in tips. Then I went back intil the shed, took aff ma dungars, went roon the back, climmed in ower the Rolls-Royce, and I wis jist drivin oot fan a twa-three o' them saw me.

'So I wound doon the windae, gied them a wave and I said: "That's me awa hame, than."

'And I could see them starin at me, and then at the car, so I jist said: "Aye, I've an affa good boss."'

The Toon

The humour of Aberdeen is quite distinct from the humour of the countryside. Toonser humour is supposedly quicker and sharper than the rural variety, which is drier and slower, although each can be either, it sometimes seems to us. Here are a few of the best examples of Granite City anecdotes that were sent to us.

SHORTLY AFTER Aberdeen set fire to its trams in that disgraceful ceremony at the beach in the early 1960s, the city's public transport became all-bus. Some of the less-swack Aberdonians complained that some of the bus platforms were too high for them to negotiate and, for several months, conductors and clippies had to bear the brunt of the moaning.

One afternoon, outside Watt and Grant's store in Union Street, a particularly fat woman was struggling to haul herself aboard.

'Come awa, mither,' said the conductor, offering her a helping haul. 'I doot ye need some yeast. It'll mak ye rise better.'

'Tak some yersel,' puffed the woman. 'It'll mak ye better-bred.'

A FIRM of Aberdeen electricians had been rewiring a council scheme on the outskirts of the city in the early 1960s and one of the sparkies, a lad so good-looking that he should have been a model or in films, had taken the fancy of a bored housewife. To the amusement of his mates, he would often repair for an hour in the afternoon to the lady's boudoir and return looking flushed, but relaxed.

One evening, back at the yard, one of the foremen shouted across to him:

'Aye, Jack, ye'll be awa back til yer new girlfriend's the nicht?'

'Na,' he called back. 'Ye dinna think I dee that kinna thing in ma ain time, d'ye?'

ONE CHRISTMAS in the early 1950s, the famed Aberdeen department store of Esslemont and Macintosh offered an embroidery service for silk stockings. Most women who took up the offer chose to have their initials or monogram embroidered around the stocking tops.

An authoritative source reports that one sparky young woman came in and asked if there would be enough room to embroider:

If you can read this, you are too close

She was being attended by two assistants, a senior man and a middle-aged woman. The man, professional to the last, didn't turn a hair and inquired simply: 'Block letters or script, madam?'

His colleague added drily: 'Or Braille, maybe?'

EVERY LORD Provost of Aberdeen dreams of the affection and regard offered to the most celebrated of his predecessors, Tommy Mitchell, who was Lord Provost during World War II. The most celebrated story, perhaps apocryphal, but with a ring of truth, tells of Lord Provost Mitchell at the Joint Station meeting the Royal Train as King George and Queen Elizabeth arrived with Princesses Elizabeth and Margaret for a short and well-earned break at Balmoral.

As the party turned to make their way from the platform, Tommy drew the Queen to one side and inquired: 'Is ony o' the twa quinies needin the lavvie?'

ONE OF Aberdeen's most notorious post-war prostitutes was spending one of her many nights in the Lodge Walk cells when, on the Sunday morning, a great racket got up as she banged a tin cup repeatedly against the cell door. During the night, her period had arrived and she bawled at the top of her voice: 'I want Tampax! I want Tampax!'

The duty officer rushed up and told her to be quiet. 'Ye'll tak porridge like a'body else.'

WHEN PROVOST Mitchell was well into his tenure, it is said that he became very concerned about the drinking of one of the city councillors, who tippled so heavily that he could become a great embarrassment on ceremonial occasions, or when dignitaries were paying official visits to Aberdeen.

At one Town House function, when a party of French politicians was being honoured with an official dinner, the councillor approached Tommy during the cocktails, before the dinner had even begun, and said: 'Well, Lord Provost, I must be saying goodbye and thank you.'

Much relieved, Tommy made a pretence of being disappointed and said: 'Must ye be awa this early?'

Then he paused. 'Or are ye bidin and jist sayin cheerio as lang ye can still recognise me?'

A RETIRED civil servant reports taking his car to one of Aberdeen's newest dealers where he sat beside a huge internal window to watch the goings-on in the service bay.

While he waited, he was struck by the work of one particular mechanic, who seemed to be more painstaking than the others.

The mechanic changed the oil without spilling a drop. He lifted the bonnet and placed the prop with the greatest care, checked the water level, then lowered the bonnet gently and clicked it shut.

Then he cleaned the windscreen and, after washing his hands, drove the car carefully out of the service-bay door and into the car park.

Just then, the service manager came to tell the customer that his car was ready.

'*I must be saying goodbye.*'

'Well,' said the customer, 'I can't help admiring the quality of that man's work. I just hope he was the man who worked on my car. I couldn't believe how careful he was with that one.'

'Aye,' said the service manager. 'That wid be because it's his.'

A RETIRED farmer had moved into one of the leafier parts of Aberdeen's West End to stay with his son and daughter-in-law and was in the habit of taking an afternoon constitutional. Not many doors up the street, a young couple had moved in and word had got around that the wife was from Stuttgart, which was enough for the old boy to go for an investigative stroll.

One afternoon, he spotted the young wife working in her front garden and he set off down his garden path, walking slowly. Once out along the pavement, he stopped beside her and leaned on her garden fence.

'Aye-aye,' he said.

She looked up into the sun, smiled and said hello.

'Ye're German,' he said.

'Well, yes, I am,' she said, and a silence hung heavily between them for a few moments.

'The Germans drappit a bomb on this street durin the war.'

She wasn't quite sure what she was supposed to say, so she waited. And he waited.

Then he stepped back and, just as he was about to leave, said: 'Dinna fash yersel. It didna ging aff.'

AN ABERDEEN taxi-driver, a Mr Duncan, was sitting in the Back Wynd taxi rank in the wee sma oors when a group of four young men, almost unconscious with drink, were led down the street by two of their slightly more sober friends.

The men collapsed into the taxi and one of the half-sober

chums leaned into the window and gave Mr Duncan a list of addresses and pointed out which drunk was to be deposited at which address.

Mr Duncan drove off but, for a bit of fun, drove round the block and back in time to see the two half-sober men still standing there, chatting to two young women. He wound down the window and called the two lads over.

'Ye hinna forgotten the addresses?' said one.

'No,' said Mr Duncan, 'could ye sort oot yer pals again? I hit a bump.'

A TORY candidate between the wars was fighting the unwinnable seat of Aberdeen North and was addressing a largely hostile meeting. One Fittie woman was particularly disparaging about Conservative policy and the party's promises for the area, and was not shy of heckling him to tell him so.

The candidate took it for so long, but eventually snapped. 'Madam,' he said, fixing her with a glare from the platform, 'you have enough brass in your neck to make a kettle.'

'Aye,' shouted the fisherwife, 'and you've enough watter in yer heid ti fill it.'

DURING THE war, Mrs Chris Clark had a job in a workmen's café with another assistant, Lizzie, who was allowed to take her four-year-old daughter, Betty, in for meals.

One day, Mrs Clark heard Betty being reprimanded for her table manners.

'Noo, Betty,' said Lizzie. 'Foo often div I hae ti tell ye? Ye dinna pit yer moo doon til the sasser fin ye drink yer tea.'

'No?'

'No. Ye lift the sasser up til yer moo.'

IN THE late 1950s, or perhaps early 1960s, the then Lord Aberdeen ventured to the telephone office in Aberdeen to pay his account. The male clerk behind the counter accepted the cheque, which had been signed 'Aberdeen'. Unfortunately, he did not recognise Lord Aberdeen and pushed the cheque back towards him, saying:

'Aye, aye, aye, we ken this is Aiberdeen. Now sign yer name.'

BILL SIVEWRIGHT and Ernie Laing were well into their eighties and were sitting in the funeral cortege in the car behind the hearse as it made its way towards the new Aberdeen Crematorium at Hazlehead.

Bill turned to Ernie and said nostalgically: 'Ernie, div ye mind fan we were young? We used to waak ahin the funeral procession. Then a puckle years efter that, we'd be in een o' the back cars. Now here we are in the car next til the hearse.'

'Aye,' said Ernie. 'We're weerin closer.'

TOMMY TOSH, now deceased, used to tell of watching the world go by at a street corner in Middlefield one day when he saw a blind man approaching, led by his guide dog. At the street corner, just a few feet from Tommy, the dog lifted its leg and urinated all over his master's trousers. The blind man felt in his pocket and took out a biscuit, which he gave to the dog.

'Aye,' said Tommy, 'I've seen some real kind things, bit that's real touchin. Yer dog peed a' ower ye and ye still gied it a biscuit.'

'Kind be damnt,' said the blind man. 'Now that I ken far his moo is, I can kick his erse.'

ADAM DUGUID, of Hazlehead, Aberdeen, reports attending a concert at the Tivoli Theatre, Aberdeen, in the early 1960s. It was a variety show, but he specifically wanted to see one of his great heroes, trombonist George Chisholm.

Adam was enjoying another masterly performance by George, when he heard the young woman sitting in front of him lean closer to the lad next to her and say: 'Is he really swallyin that thing?'

WHEN JACK Robertson, of Middlefield, ran out of cigarettes at the Fish Market one day, he asked a fellow-porter for a match, thinking that that would spur the man into offering a cigarette, too.

Jack took the offered match, patted his overalls and said: 'Dash it, I doot I've left ma fags at hame, as weel.'

The colleague reached over. 'In that case,' he said. 'Ye winna be needin the match.'

The Papers

If an area is reflected best by its newspapers, then the North-east can claim a healthy clutch of weeklies, but principally the Press and Journal *and* Evening Express. *It's not generally appreciated that the* Press and Journal *is the highest-circulation regional morning paper, not just in Britain, but throughout the UK; it is one of the three oldest English-language papers in the world, and far outstrips the* Scotsman, Herald, Yorkshire Post *and other dailies that spring to mind. Now that the shameless plugging is over, here are a few tales shared by North-east journalists present and past.*

WHEN A writer from the *Press and Journal* was dispatched to tell first-year pupils at Turriff Academy about life as a journalist, the class sat dutifully through his talk as he explained about training, use of English, knowledge of law, an ability to get on with people, persistence and long hours.

When he finished, he invited questions, but, as in many North-east schools, the class was too shy. Despite repeated requests, no one could be persuaded to ask anything.

The *P&J*'s man decided to go into a little of the history of the paper, for it's not commonly understood that the *Press and Journal* is the third-oldest English-language newspaper in the world. He explained that it had been established in December, 1747, and had published its first copy in January, 1748. It had been founded by a man called James Chalmers.

At that, a ripple of laughter started in one of the back corners and many others in the class turned to see what was happening.

'What is it?' asked the *P&J* man. 'Have I said something funny?'

'No,' said one of the class pointing at a fellow-pupil, 'but his name's Chalmers.'

'Oh, well,' said the *P&J* man. 'It could even be that the P. and J. was founded by one of your ancestors.'

'Nuh,' said the pupil in question.

'Oh, but how can you be so sure?'

'Hinna got ony ancestors.'

AT ANOTHER schools talk, the same writer invited questions and, again, no one could be persuaded out of their shyness. 'Come on, now,' he said. 'Surely someone has a question.'

Eventually, a shy little thing in the front row put up her hand.

'Yes,' he said. 'What would you like to know.'

'Far did ye get yer sheen?' she asked in a very small voice.

'My shoes?' he said, trying not to look surprised. 'Well, I think it was a shop at Inverurie. Why? Do you like them?'

She looked at the shoes and then looked up at him.

'Nae really.'

THE SAME writer was dispatched to a Donside school to talk to pupils there and found them in the middle of a maths lesson. Being a forward-looking school, the maths lesson took a practical form. The teacher had written out a cake recipe and had asked the pupils to work out a proportion sum by converting a recipe for 10 servings to a recipe for 16.

To test their skills, the cake had been baked. As guest for the afternoon, the *Press and Journal*'s man was invited to cut the cake and sample the first slice, so he pointedly made a fuss of how tasty it was.

Then teacher invited all the others in the class to have a piece, and all clamoured forward. All apart from one boy, who stood at the back, not eating.

'What's the matter?' said the *Press and Journal*'s man, 'are you not having a slice of your delicious cake?'

'Na,' he said. 'I ken fit I put in it.'

THE SAME man reports attending a small WRI in the middle of Aberdeenshire, again for the purposes of giving a talk. After speaking for 40 minutes, he was invited to take tea with the committee. Somehow – he is not entirely sure – a strip of raffle tickets appeared at his side and, worried in case someone had mislaid them, he drew the president to one side and pointed them out.

'Na, na,' she said. 'That's your strippie, that. We aye buy a strippie for wir guest spikker.'

He thanked her kindly and sat back, waiting for the numbers to be drawn.

Then she stepped back towards him and said: 'And we hope ye dinna win.'

ONE MORNING in the mid-1980s, all the radio-network wavelengths in North-east Scotland changed to try to tidy up the airwaves. Realising that great confusion was likely as the region tried to retune thousands of radios, the BBC and the IBA had been plugging the changeover for weeks and, on the Monday morning, the *Press and Journal* published a big notice explaining as much.

Shortly after 12.30pm, the features editor of the paper took a call from a very frail, elderly voice. 'I canna find Robbie Shepherd,' she wailed.

'Well, all the radio stations changed today,' said the features editor. 'Have you retuned your radio?'

'Oh, I did hear something aboot that, bit I dinna ken nithing aboot radios,' she said.

'All right. All right,' said the features editor. 'Do you have your paper in front of you?'

'Aye.'

'Is it open at the TV page?'

'Aye.'

'And do you see where it says Radio Aberdeen?'

'Na. I ken fit I put in it.'

'Aye.'

'Do you see a three-figure number next to Radio Aberdeen?'

'Aye.'

'Well, if you turn the dial on your radio to where it says that three-figure number, you'll get Robbie Shepherd.'

'Bit I dinna think it says onything on ma radio.'

'Does it not say anything on the top of your radio?'

'Wait a mintie.' And he heard the sound of footsteps walking slowly over to the other side of the room. A few seconds later, they returned and the phone was lifted.

'No, it disna say nithing on the top o' ma radio.'

'Does it not say anything on the front of your radio, then?'

'Jist a mintie.' And the footsteps went off again.

Back they came. 'No, it disna say nithing on the front o' ma radio, eether.'

'Well, what about the back of your radio?'

'Jist a mintie.' Off she went and back she came, this time with a note of triumph in her voice.

'Yes, it dis say something on the back o' ma radio.'

'What does it say?'

'Made in Taiwan.'

THE FAREWELL gift is a tradition in offices up and down the land but journalism, in which the pool of available professional talent is remarkably small, frequently sees careers move in spirals, with some hacks returning to the scenes of their cub days before moving onward and upward yet again.

The *Press and Journal* was home to one particularly nomadic chap, who stayed for a few months, moved on, and returned every couple of years to stay for several more months, before moving on, and so on.

Each time, a whipround provided him with a handsome farewell gift until, on the fourth occasion, the large buff envelope presented to a particularly gruff sports writer brought a curt wave-away and: 'Season ticket.'

JIMMY GRANT was one of the most celebrated journalists the North-east has ever produced, and was editor of the *Press and Journal* until he retired in 1975. Once invited to a garden party at Holyroodhouse, he accepted, but was determined not to be outdone by the great and the good who, he knew, would be sporting chestfuls of medals.

On the day in question, Jimmy turned up wearing a large silvery medallion which impressed all who saw him. It caused great interest, and when one acquaintance bumped into him and commented on it, he winked and held it out for study.

It had belonged to his mother, as the legend explained:

Turriff Show. Best Butter. 1933.

ONE YOUNG journalist once asked Jimmy Grant why so many people bought the *Press and Journal* in small country villages and towns when, one would expect, everyone knew everyone else's business, anyway.

'Aye,' said Jimmy, 'they do. But they read the paper to see fa's been caught at it.'

A FORMER *Evening Express* reporter remembers going to a tenement in Torry to interview a former fisherman who had reached the ripe old age of 100. As is customary, he asked the birthday boy to what he attributed his old age.

The man thought for quite a while and said: 'Faith in the Lord. Get up early. Dinna sweir. Dinna drink. And dinna smoke.'

The reporter duly noted all this down, saying: 'Well, that's marvellous. Mind you, I had an uncle at Elgin and that was exactly the way he lived and he died at eighty-two. How do you account for that?'

'Aweel,' grinned the fisherman. 'He surely didna keep it up lang enough.'

ONE OF the facts of newspaper life is that everyone will disagree with something. Some say that a newspaper that doesn't annoy a good few of its readers every morning isn't doing its job properly. These days, provided that a complaint is genuine and proven, any newspaper will do its best to correct any error for which it is responsible.

The complaints which are merely differences of opinion are another matter. In these days of customer care, readers whose complaints are merely prejudices will be let down as gently as possible and told why a 'correction' is not possible – because nothing was wrong in the first place.

It was not always so gentle. One editor of a daily paper happened to be passing the newsdesk phone ringing one evening and picked it up. He was treated to a tirade of abuse for the coverage of what had seemed a perfectly innocent report of a minor political meeting. The caller felt that his party had not been given due credit and space. The editor, whose job it is to decide who gets what coverage, listened stoically while an aspiring politician lectured him on how to do his job.

He tried several times to interrupt and explain the paper's policy, but the party man was determined to have his say. Eventually, the editor decided to wait for the flow of invective to falter, then said: 'Excuse me, do you know who you're talking to?'

'I do not.'

'Then bugger off.'

A PRESS and Journal man was dispatched to a schools careers evening at Inverurie Academy and was duly manning the stand when an extremely reluctant and gangly youth was propelled towards him by a portly gent with the ruddy face and gnarled hands of a man of the soil.

The *Press and Journal* man took them for farmer father and son.

He went through a five-minute explanation of the demands of the job, the qualifications needed and how competitive it was even to get a place on a training programme, let alone a job. Then he asked if the boy had any questions.

'Go on, Gordon,' said the farmer. 'The blokie's askin if ye've a question. Speir awa.'

Gordon did not look up, but mumbled a good North-east question: 'Fit's the siller like?' The *Press and Journal* man explained the salary scales and merit awards, trainee indentures and senior-journalist rates.

'And foo muckle div you mak?' asked Gordon.

The *Press and Journal* man gave his stock answer: 'Well,' he said. 'More than a pittance, but not quite as much as a fortune.'

This time, the father leaned forward, with a farmer's gleam in his eye:

'And foo muckle's that exactly?'

THEY SAY in the Classified Advertising department of Aberdeen Journals that during a sales promotion offering seven words for £2, a Buchan family phoned up to place a death notice and suggested as wording:

'John Reid. Bogheid. Deid.'

'Well, yes,' said the tele-ad girl, 'but that's only four words and you can have seven for your two pounds.'

'We'll phone ye back,' said the family.

Five minutes later, the phone rang again.

'Right, we've sortit it oot. We'll say:

'John Reid. Bogheid. Deid. Volvo for sale.'

Aches and Pains

The doctor, one of the honoured North-east triumvirate which includes dominie and minister, is held in great respect in villages and towns throughout the North-east to this day. This privileged position gives a doctor a marvellous perspective for seeing North-east wit at its most unwitting.

THE DOCTOR at Tarland, shortly after World War I, was called to the deathbed of a farmer's wife near Coull. The lady was in great pain and it became clear very quickly that there was little that he could do except make her more comfortable. The farmer, a stocky, unexpressive man, stared solidly from the foot of the bed. Three hours later, the lady breathed her last, the doctor performed the duties necessary and the farmer, quite out of character, broke down in tears and fell to his knees.

Three days after the funeral, the doctor met the farmer in the street at Tarland and said: 'In view of your bereavement, I'm prepared to forget about half my bill.'

'That's rale decent o' ye, doctor,' said the farmer. 'And seein as it's yersel, I'll forget aboot the ither half.'

SHORTLY AFTER Aberdeen's spanking new Royal Infirmary was opened in the mid-1930s (largely by public subscription, which gives the lie to the North-east reputation for grip), a workman's bothy caught fire at the eastern end of the site.

Rather than cause a panic in the nearest wards, nursing sisters instructed their staff to draw screens round the beds so that patients need not become overwrought.

One patient who came round after an operation saw the screens and asked: 'Fit wye the screens? Did ye nae expect me ti recover?'

'No,' said the nurse. 'It's nae that. A bothy ootside the

'Fit wye the screens?'

windae catched fire and we didna wint ye ti see the flames
and think the worst hid happened.'

ONE RETIRED Donside doctor reports a tale from his
days as a medical student at Aberdeen University, when
a tutor inquired of his tutor group if any of them intended
to specialise.

'Oh, yes, indeed,' said one ambitious young Englishman.
'I feel the area that will offer the most interesting medical
advances in future will be the diseases of the nose. Most
certainly.'

'I see,' said the weary old doctor. 'Just the nose? Not
Ear, Nose and Throat?'

'Just the nose,' confirmed the student grandly. 'I feel that
the ears and throat are too complicated to be combined
with the nose for the purposes of study and treatment.'

'Hmm,' said the old doctor. 'And will you concentrate
on any nostril in particular?'

A SMALL boy who was exceptionally keen on fishing had
managed to get a hook fouled in his hand and was taken
to the doctor to have the hook removed.

The doctor managed the operation reasonably quickly
and, as mother and son made towards the door, he noticed
that the boy was hanging back. 'Is there something else?'
he asked the boy.

'Aye,' said the lad. 'Gies back ma hook.'

DURING THE war, men of a certain age had to go through
a medical before being enlisted. The medical panel came
across one chap they thought was skiving and decided to
try to catch him out.

'What is the time on that clock, Mr D——?' they
inquired.

He looked at the clock and replied: 'Couldna tell ye. The

only time I ken is fan the twa hans is at the top, and that's dennertime.'

DR DANNY Gordon was a country doctor who practised at Ellon for many years and was held in the highest regard. He used to tell a story, from pre-NHS days, of how he was called out to a confinement and it was to be the arrival of a fifth child to a Mrs MacGregor.

The midwife was waiting anxiously by the front door.

'Fit ail't ye, doctor, and Mrs MacGregor wytin sair for ye?'

Dr Danny made little comment, but went about his own couthy but professional way.

'What kept me?' he used to chuckle many years later. 'I could have said plenty, bit I wis there in time for the call o' duty and, to tell ye the truth, I hidna been peyed for the safe arrival o' the ither fower.'

AUL RIDDELL was a gamekeeper on a Donside estate just after the war and was persuaded by his wife, after much pressure and nagging, to visit the doctor to see about his shortness of breath and stomach pains. After 70 years of never a day's illness, he knew himself he wasn't any longer in the best of condition. He wasn't able to tramp the hills in pursuit of the grouse, and was beginning to fail in his duties in organising a shoot.

After the usual examination and questions about lifestyle, the doctor got to the truth of the matter. Putting the stethoscope aside, he felt around the gamie's rotund frame and sighed.

'I suggest, Mr Riddell, that you'll have to cut out the drink and the cigarettes.'

Looking up from the couch, the gamie grunted and mused. 'I see. I see. And hiv ye a knife, doctor?'

The doctor, somewhat taken aback, asked why.

'Because if ye're makkin me dee athoot ma drink and

ma fags, ye micht as weel cut aff the mannie and get rid o' a' ma pleesures at the same time.'

IN THE days before the National Health Service, not a million miles from the Cabrach, Dr Scott was called to attend a farmhouse where a young maidservant seemed to be suffering from severe depression.

On arriving, the good doctor tried out the psychology and experience of a rural practitioner – the techniques these kindly men had in abundance. After a lengthy chat in his best bedside manner, he realised that the kitchie deem had simply taken to bed in the sulks because the farmer had not paid her wages for five or six weeks. It was an early and inspired form of industrial action.

'I'll lie him oot,' she confided. 'He'll pey up afore I tak ma body aff this bed.'

'Noo lassie,' said the soothing tones of the doctor. 'Jist ee lie ower a bittie and I'll get in aside ye. He hisna peyed me, eether.'

THIS ONE comes from a relative of one of your co-authors' families. Aunt Mary was a nurse and on duty in the out-patient's department of Aberdeen Royal Infirmary. An elderly lady, a litttle confused, was ushered into the ward, told to lie down on the bed and the consultant would be round to visit her shortly.

Along came the man of authority and, with the screens round about the bed, he started the usual pleasantries with a remark on how well she was getting on.

'Now,' he said gently, 'if you would just take down your pants.'

There was no response; not even a flicker of an eyelid from the old lady on the bed.

'I say, please take down your pants.'

Still nothing.

After repeating the request at least twice more, the

exasperated consultant was almost shouting when he said: 'Mrs B——, I have a long list of patients in front of me and I really must hurry you up. Will you please take down your knickers?'

The woman on the bed finally stirred.

'Oh, I'm affa sorry, doctor. Are ye spikkin ti me? I thocht ye wis spikkin til the nursie here.'

IT WAS the first time in hospital for old Willie. He had never had a day's illness in his life but then, without warning, he was felled by a stroke. The first few days in hospital were a blur, but then he recovered sufficiently to play his part in the daily ritual of hospital life.

Wakened at the crack of dawn, as is the wont of nursing staff, he was surprised to find the curtains drawn round about him, with a cheery nurse beside him with a basin full of steaming hot water and all the required toiletries.

'Now, Willie, ye're gettin a bed-bath.'

'Michty, nursie,' said Willie. 'Ye'll nivver get ma erse in that sma basin.'

THE NEXT three are not so much Dashes of Doric, but they are all genuine transcriptions of reports from Aberdeen Royal Infirmary, as told to us by a receptionist.

1. A doctor had dictated on his machine: 'The old man was admitted with severe lower abdominal pain due to constipation.' The resulting transcription read: 'The old man was admitted with severe lower abdominal pain due to constant passion.'

2. A phone call from a GP to the hospital stated that: 'The patient's got a renal colic', which was transcribed into the daily written report for hospital staff as: 'The patient's a real wee comic.'

3. Again from a rural doctor: 'My patient, I'm sure,

has a chest complaint, perhaps emphysematous.' This was transcribed on the word-processor as: 'My patient, I'm sure, has a chest complaint, perhaps with his semmit on.'

Law and Order

We have included this chapter to prove that even lawyers, judges and policemen have a sense of humour. Unfortunately, the planned chapter on accountants had to go by the board.

ONE ABERDEEN lawyer between the wars used to tell a deliciously self-deprecating story of walking down Union Street, Aberdeen, with his wife one Sunday when a voluptuous young blonde whom he had managed to defend successfully in court, shouted and waved a cheery wave and blew him a kiss across the street.

He waved back before he realised that his wife was glowering.

'She was that case a few months back,' he said hastily. 'And before you ask it was purely a professional relationship.'

'Aye,' said his wife. 'Your profession or hers?'

SHERIFF MUIR Russell was one of the more entertaining dispensers of justice at Aberdeen Sheriff Court. One one occasion, passing a sentence of two years' imprisonment on a notorious old thief and drunk in his 70s, the guilty man wailed: 'I'll nivver live ti finish twa years ma lord.'

'Never mind,' said Sheriff Russell. 'Just you do what you can.'

SHERIFF RUSSELL was also in situ when a young hooligan was being fined £50 for breaking the peace. 'Do you need time to pay?' inquired the sheriff.

The youth, either sullen or unable to understand the question, stood there glowering silently.

'Do you need time to pay your fine in instalments?' inquired Sheriff Russell again.

The youth stood in glum silence.

Eventually, the sheriff addressed the court. 'Is there anyone present who can speak for this young man?' A middle-aged man in anorak and jeans stood and raised his hand. 'I'm his da, yer lordship.' Sheriff Russell beckoned him down and the man stood beside his son.

'I was asking,' said Sheriff Russell, 'if your son needed time to pay his fine in instalments. I shall assume that he does. Now, would five pounds per week be in order?'

The man and his son went into a huddle of intense discussion, which broke a few seconds later and the father announced: 'No, yer lordship, not acceptable. I'm sorry.'

'What?' said Sheriff Russell, 'an apprentice tradesman with a reputable city firm and he can't manage five pounds a week? Why ever not?'

'Be fair, sir,' said the father. 'Fags and drink's an affa price nooadays.'

ONE BRIGHT spark at the Tulliallan Police College was asked what action he would take to help disperse a crowd.

'Well,' he said. 'In Aiberdeen, we'd start a collection.'

IN THE 1940s, James Simpson, a Banff solicitor, had an office at Foggieloan, where he did a few hours' consulting each week. A Foggie couple called one afternoon to arrange a defence on a charge of poultry-stealing. They sat down and gave an account of the incident, which Mr Simpson began to ponder.

He sat pensively with his elbows on the desk and his head cupped in his hands, eyes closed, considering the best course of action. He must have been sitting that way for a good few minutes – certainly longer than he realised – because he was startled to hear the wife say:

'Come on hame, Jim. The bugger's sleepin.'

MARY HAD a shoppie in a small Buchan village. One

How to disperse a crowd in Aberdeen

night, it was raided and the drawers ransacked. The village bobby arrived the following morning to make inquiries and, not noted for his sensitivity, asked: 'Weel, Mary, so somebody wis interferin wi yer drawers last nicht, eh?'

TWO BOBBIES were attending a road accident at a country crossroads which, in those days, was bounded on all sides by drystane dykes. The driver of one car, an old Austin Seven, said he had not seen the other car coming because of the height of the dyke.

The bobby was suspicious, and thought that the driver should certainly have been able to see the other car coming, because the driver's seat in an Austin Seven was not that low. But how could he prove it?

Shortly, he hit on a plan. He squatted down in the middle of the road and said to his colleague: 'Measure the distance fae the grun til my erse, then we'll measure the hicht o' his seat fae the grun. Then we'll fin oot whither he saw the car or no.'

MANY YEARS ago, there worked in Aberdeen a police inspector who stood no nonsense from lower ranks and who never missed an opportunity to put them on the spot. One day, he was out in a patrol car with his driver, as well as a crewman and beatman in the back seat.

A call came over the radio. 'Control calling East Car! Control calling East Car! Go right away to the Boathouse Briggie. There's kids throwing stones at the trains.'

'Roger,' said the inspector.

Eager to impress his three colleagues with his knowledge of the city, he asked the driver: 'Do you know where the Boathouse Briggie is?'

'No,' said the driver, honestly.

He turned to the crewman. 'Do you?'

'No, sir.'

He turned to Peter, the beatman, convinced that total

victory would soon be his. 'And you, Peter? Do you know where the Boathouse Briggie is?'

'Aye,' said Peter.

A fleeting look of disappointment crossed the inspector's face. 'Far is it, than?'

'It's far the kids is throwin steens at the trains.'

CONGRATULATIONS TO John Stewart, formerly of Grampian Police, who had the guts to tell a fine story against himself. When he was a beat bobby in the Mastrick and Northfield districts of Aberdeen, he covered his area on a bike – a great, black monster of a bike, he reports, with a seat like a Fordson Tractor.

One snowy day, he was cycling round the Cornhill prefabs and noticed a group of children enjoying themselves sledging down a short slope. However, John spotted that the slope ended beside a busy road, and he was concerned that an accident would occur.

He rode his big, black cycle towards them, intending to point out the dangers very gently. When he was about 20 yards from them, they became aware of him, stopped their sledging and gathered into a little guilty huddle at the foot of the icy slope.

'Now, kids,' he shouted, still cycling. 'You shouldn't be sledging here. It's dangerous.'

At the precise moment of uttering the word 'dangerous', the bike skidded from under him and he travelled the last few yards flat on his back and into the group of children. He looked up at a sea of frightened and innocent faces. And all he could think of to say was:

'Ye see fit I mean?'

BOB MILNE was butcher at Dunecht for many years and ran three vans delivering all round the area. He was out in one of them every day of the week, and it meant long hours. As is the way of country mobile shoppies, he was more than just a butcher; he carried news and did messages and all sorts of other community good deeds that go unsung too often. As a genial character, he was often invited into homes for a fly cup and news, or perhaps something stronger in the bitter days of winter.

There was a by-law at the time that prevented a vanman blowing his whistle to give notice of his arrival after 8pm. The Echt bobby had warned Bob many times, but Bob needed to speed up his rounds late in the day and the whistle was the only way to do it.

One night at Echt, Bob fussled his fussle once too often and the bobby stormed out of the station and up to the van: 'Dammit, butcher,' he said, 'I've tellt ye again and again tae tak that infernal fussle oot o' yer moo at this time o' nicht, and eneuch's eneuch. I maun chairge ye.'

An hour later, Bob was still delivering, this time at Midmar, just two or three miles up the road from Echt. The last delivery was a parcel of beef to the hostelry at Midmar – at the time licensed only for beer. As usual, Bob made his way into the kitchen for his nightcap to find the self-same bobby plunkit down at the table, diced cap on his knee and a liberal dram of whisky in his hand.

Revenge, when it comes, comes swiftly.

'Aye, aye, bobby,' said Bob. 'I didna ken the law allowed ye ti drink fusky in a porter and ale hoose.'

Bob was never charged.

IT'S A hot day at Aberdeen Beach and one bobby is striding along the Esplanade licking surreptitiously at an ice-cream cappie while enjoying the balmy breezes. Unfortunately for him and for his career prospects, the inspector is out on the prowl and spots his constable in a near-deserted part of the Esplanade carrying an ice-cream cone.

He directs the driver to draw up beside the constable.

'Now, min,' said the inspector. 'Ye ken fine ye shouldna be aetin an ice-cream on duty. I dinna care foo het it is. And fit the hell are ye deein awa up at this end, onywye? There's nithing up here. You should be doon at the ither end, in amon the folk, spikkin til them and makkin yersel seen.'

'Oh, aye, sir,' said the bobby, licking the rapidly melting remains of his ice-cream while being reprimanded. 'I tak yer pint. Fairly that. Aye.'

'Well, than, awa ye go,' said the inspector. 'And dinna let it happen again, or we'll hae ti see aboot it, and I'll mind on this caper the day wi yer ice-cream.'

'Aye, sir,' said the bobby. 'Fairly that. I tak yer pint.'

Then the bobby stopped. 'Eh, there's jist ae thing, sir.'

'And fit's that?' said the inspector.

The bobby popped the last of the cone into his mouth and swallowed it.

'Far's yer evidence?'

THERE IS a hardy annual story among the boys and girls in blue at Grampian Police of the slow-witted North-east cadet sent off for training to the police college. He was struggling with the phonetic alphabet (A Alpha, B Bravo, C Charlie, and so on), and was asked in a rapid-fire, random question session in class what the E stood for.

Quick as a flash, he shouted: 'Aeple.'

THE LAST winter before the Kittybrewster Mart closed in Aberdeen, two farmers from Insch and Kennethmont were heard discussing how sharp the frosts had been, and the Insch man wondered if this wasn't the coldest winter they could remember?

'Nivver,' said the Kennethmont man, 'div ye nae mind the winter o' 1947?'

'Wis it caul?'

'Caul? I'll say it wis caul. Ma wife saw twa solicitors walkin doon Union Street and they'd their hands in their ain pooches.'

Please, Miss

Of all the professions, the one that has the most profound effect on any community is the teacher. Teacher's grip lasts a lifetime, well after the confines of the classroom. But even teachers have a sense of humour. In fact, it's probably a professional necessity.

A TEACHER who spent a large part of his career at Ellon Academy recalls marking an exercise in which one of the questions had been: 'What is rabies and what can you do about it?'

One answer was: 'Rabies is Jewish ministers. You can't do anything about it.'

A PRIMARY teacher in a North-east rural school was having terrible trouble stopping one of her broader-spoken pupils from using the word 'putten' when, as we all know, the word is 'put'.

To correct him once and for all, she wrote on the board:

I have just putten on my shoes

. . . then asked him if he saw anything wrong with the sentence.

'Aye,' he said confidently, 'ye've gaen and putten putten far ye should hiv putten put.'

A TEACHER at a primary school in Upper Donside was having quite a job persuading one young farmer's son to speak English and not lapse into the Doric. The last straw came one afternoon when they were discussing parents' hobbies.

'Ma mither maks her ain wine,' he told the class. 'Bit she's hid ti stop for a file, for she hisna nae bottles.'

'No, no, no, no, no,' said the teacher, standing up. 'Not:

The putten down

"She hisna nae bottles." It should be. "My mother has no bottles." Now, start again.'

He began again, treading a little more warily. 'My mother makes wine but she has had to stop for a while because she has no bottles.'

'Much better,' said the teacher approvingly. 'Anything else?'

'Aye,' said the boy. 'She's gey ticht for corks, tee.'

TWIN brothers were sitting in a circle of fellow-pupils during a primary-school reading lesson. They stuck at the word GRACE. The teacher tried to coax one of them out of the stall, saying: 'Come on, now, Robbie. What does your father say before a meal?'

Robbie looked at Frankie and Frankie looked at Robbie.

Robbie looked at the teacher. 'Please, miss, ma faither says: "Robbie and Frunkie, blaa yer noses."'

MISS MACKIE taught near Monymusk in the early 1950s and was annoyed one day when two small brothers turned up late for school. Miss Mackie asked the older one why.

'Well, Miss,' he said, 'I was half-way to the school but I took an awful sair belly and had to run intil the woods.'

'I see,' said Miss Mackie, turning to the smaller boy, 'and what about you, Sandy, did you have a sore stomach, too?'

'No, miss,' said Sandy, 'bit I hid ti pu the grass.'

MANY YEARS ago, the bakery at Tarland was Grant's the Bakers. The infant class at school were working their way through a lesson about animal noises. The cow moos. The sheep baas, the pig grunts.

'Now,' said the teacher, 'does anyone have a story about moos, or baas or grunts?'

'Please, miss,' said one lad, 'I get ma playpiece fae Grunts.'

JAMES MICHIE, long-time director of education in Aberdeenshire and then for Grampian Region, and an ardent proponent of the Doric, tells a delicious story of paying an official visit to Braemar Primary School and accepting the teacher's offer of keeping his hand in by teaching a class of eight-year-olds for a short time.

Mr Michie enjoyed the 40 minutes back at the blackboard thoroughly, and asked the boys and girls if they had, too.

'Oh, yes, sir,' they chorused.

Mr Michie thanked them all and began walking towards the classroom door when a small voice piped from the back: 'Hey, min, ye're awa wi wir chalk.'

AT THE handwork class, a teacher not from the North-east was having difficulty getting the boys, in particular, to hurry up making placemats by threading laces through holes in pieces of card.

Eventually, she said: 'Come on, Ian; hurry up threading that lace through those holes.'

Ian looked at her thoughtfully. 'That's nae lace. That's pints.'

THE SAME Ian was listening to the same teacher telling the Bible story about the lost sheep. She told the class that the wee lamb had said to itself that it would leave the other lambs and go on to the rocks and explore, and that was why it got lost. 'Now,' she said to the class, 'what do you think of that?'

'I dinna believe it,' said Ian. 'Sheep canna spik.'

AT GALLOWHILL School, a small boy wandered into the headmaster's room. 'Are ee the dominie, sir?'

'I am.'

'Div you ken this: the grieve shot oor cat last nicht.'

'Oh, my, that's a terrible shame. Did you cry?'

'Fit wid I dee that for? It wis the cat he shot, nae me.'

PUPILS ARRIVED at Rhynie School as usual one morning and sat down in their usual places, except for one older boy who stood. The teacher told him to sit down.

He said he couldn't, because 'if ee'd a blin lump on yer erse as I hiv, ee'd be gled ti stan, tee.'

FORMER TEACHER turned writer Lilianne Grant Rich tells of six-year-old Robbie, who came from one of the outlying crofts and had to walk two miles to school and two miles back every day. Lilianne was in no doubt that Robbie was turned out impeccably by his mother every morning but, by the time he had investigated all the dykes and burns and ditches on the two miles, he arrived always in need of a good encounter with soap and water.

Although he said nothing, Robbie's face for the first few mornings in Lilianne's class indicated that he regarded the calling of the class roll a daft-like ploy and that he, for one, would have nothing to do with it if at all possible.

For a week, Lilianne ignored it, thinking that he would soon feel left out and would want to join in like the others.

Then, one day, she called his name three times, fixing him with a stare.

Eventually, and extremely reluctantly, Robbie said: 'Present.'

Lilianne noted it with satisfaction.

'Aye,' said Robbie, 'bit ye saw me a' the time.'

THE SAME Robbie was in class one wintry morning during hymn-singing. As Lilianne played piano, Robbie rose from his seat and strode over to the classroom fire and stretched his hands to the blaze.

She took no notice for a few moments, but eventually stopped in mid-verse and looked towards him inquiringly.

A few moments later, Robbie realised she had stopped playing. He gave her a brief glance over his right shoulder and said, in a completely matter-of-fact and reassuring way: 'Aye, on ye go wi yer playin. Nivver heed me. I'm fair frozen.'

ROBBIE HAD difficulty with arithmetic, and no matter how Lilianne tried to explain to him that a number subtracted from itself left nothing, he couldn't grasp it at all. She tried counters, dots and fingers, but it just wouldn't sink in. Eventually, summoning another waucht of patience, she said: 'Now, Robbie, we'll pretend it's market day. You have six pigs at home and I'm going to take a lorry and take six pigs away. How many would be left?'

At last, a look of radiant understanding illuminated Robbie's face. 'Man,' he said, 'that wid be gran. There wid be neen left, and I could bide in ma bed til eicht ilky mornin, for I wid hae nithing ti feed bit masel and ma rubbits.'

ONE WEEK, Robbie arrived late every morning, and Lilianne began to wonder if he was taking a dislike to school. As the bairns were leaving for home on the Friday afternoon, she said with a laugh: 'Well, Robbie, do you think you'll be on time for school on Monday?'

'No, I dinna think so,' he said. 'Ye see, I *div* like ti come in late and get a "Good Morning, Robbie" a' til masel.'

IN ANOTHER of Lilianne's classes was Jean, a small chatterbox, almost to the point of disruption. In those days, removal of tonsils and adenoids was not as common as it is today and Jean went round bragging about her forthcoming visit to hospital. Some weeks later, she was back in her usual place, blethering non-stop.

Sandy, who shared her desk, looked up imploringly at

Lilianne and said with a sigh that indicated real disappointment: 'Yon doctor mannie maybe took Jean's tonsils awa, bit I'll sweir he nivver took her tongue.'

ONE MONTH, the headmaster delivered the teachers' pay cheques personally, and laid Lilianne's on her desk.

Billy interrupted. 'That's yer pey, isn't it?'

Lilianne just nodded.

Billy thought for a few moments more. 'My dad gies me tippence a wikk. Foo muckle dis he (with a jerk of his head towards the headmaster) gie you?'

LILIANNE ADMITTED to the butterflies all teachers experience when HM Inspectorate pays a visit to the classroom, but was charmed when six-year-old Valerie was standing beside one inspector, reading to him, when the inspector took hold of one of her gorgeous red curls and pretended to cut it off and put it in his pocket.

Valerie laid down her book and contemplated him closely for a moment. Then, taking him by both lapels, she gave him a gentle shake and said: 'Oh, my! Fit'll we dee wi this great big coorse loon?'

DAISY WISEMAN was a teacher at Folla Rule School between the wars and used to tell of a farmer's son, Jimmy Grant, who was among the new intake listening to her explaining about the standards of behaviour she would expect from them.

Suddenly, Jimmy rose from his seat and stamped towards the door. 'And where might you be going?' asked his teacher.

'Nivver you mind,' said Jimmy. 'I'll be back in twa ticks.'

Sure enough, Jimmy was back two minutes later and said to Miss Wiseman.

''At's better. I wis fair burstin.'

AT WOODLANDS School on Lower Deeside in 1944, the class was having a geography lesson from their teacher, Miss Spark, when the dominie, Mr McKelvie, appeared and said to one pupil: 'Geography is it, James? All right, then, can you tell me what a cape is?'

'Yes, sir,' said James. 'It's a cap ye weir on yer heid.'

IT WAS coming up for the annual school concert at a Buchan primary school. We believe it was at Longside, but we can't be absolutely certain. The teacher in Primary One was holding informal auditions for a farmyard scene as a backdrop to the nativity play.

'Now, who can do farmyard noises?'

Up shot a few eager hands. 'Please, miss, I can moo,' said Jean.

'I can clock lik a hen,' said Annie.

'Me, miss! I can grunt lik a pig,' cried Airchie.

'And I can baa,' said Tommy.

Then up shot the hand of wee Johnnie, whose domain was his father's farm.

'All right, Johnnie,' said the teacher. 'Let's hear your farmyard noise.'

'Get aff that bliddy tractor!'

SOMETIMES, TEACHERS don't get the answers they expect. One woman in charge of a primary class, who asked not to be named or credited, asked in the late 1940s for a sentence using the word 'exaggeration'.

A hand went up. 'Please, miss, my faither says ye're guid-lookin, bit ma mither says that's an exaggeration.'

Good for the Soul

As in many other areas of Scotland, the minister is still regarded as one of the three buttresses of community; the others being the dominie and the doctor. Most of the stories in this section came from ministers themselves, all of whom requested that they stay anonymous, which goes to show, we suppose, that a dog-collar and a sense of humour are not mutually exclusive.

A KINCARDINE minister was also a keen golfer and had accepted an invitation for a Saturday round of golf at Inverurie. Unfortunately, the minister was playing very badly and was becoming more and more frustrated until, by the time he missed an easy putt at the 14th, he could contain himself no longer and let go a minor expletive or two.

His golfing chum – also a member of his flock – was mildly shocked that a man of the cloth had such a ripe vocabulary, and said as much.

'You're quite right, of course, Peter,' said the minister. 'In fact, I've been thinking for a while that I'm going to have to give up the whole thing. It's just getting too frustrating for me.'

The chum was just as horrified. 'Michty,' he said, 'surely ye widna gie up yer golf?'

'Certainly not,' said the minister. 'I meant the ministry.'

OLD MAGGIE had forgotten to put her clock forward an hour at the end of March and arrived an hour late at the kirk. She stepped down the aisle in a fine new hat just as the minister raised his arms and pronounced: 'Jesus Christ! Hallelujah!' at the end of the service. Maggie about-turned and marched out.

The minister became worried when Maggie did not turn

The Sunday golfer

up for the next few weeks, so he visited her and asked why she wasn't in church these days.

'Weel, minister,' she said, 'the last time I turned up ye raised yer hauns and cried: "Jesus Christ, I hardly knew ye!" and that wis an affa thing to say aboot ma new hat.'

ONE WEARY minister at Forglen had noted that a spate of break-ins around the parish had happened over the weekend and had caused great concern. After the Sunday service, he was chatting to parishioners when one elder asked: 'What would you do, minister, if someone broke into the manse one night looking for money?'

'Well,' said the minister, 'I'd rise and help him.'

A FORMER prison chaplain at Peterhead noticed that one of the prisoners never received any visitors and, as the weeks wore on, began to feel mightily sorry for him.

'Tell me, Jim,' he said one day. 'I notice that nobody ever comes to visit you. Have you no friends or family?'

'Aye,' said Jim, 'bit they're a' in the jile, as weel.'

A COUNTRY woman who had moved into a granite villa in the West End of Aberdeen after her husband had shown a talent at playing the stock market was about to be visited by the new minister. Unfortunately, a gang of ruffians was playing about in the street outside.

The lads began taunting the minister for his odd style of dress and for having a very old car. The minister (the man who wrote to tell us about the story) was quite amused by it and chose to sail through it towards the front door, but his hostess-to-be was horrified, and lost no time in telling the ruffians so.

Unfortunately, she made the common mistake of trying to pan-loaf it.

'You! You ruffians! Get away with you! Away home to your mithers! I'll call the police!'

Then she turned to the minister and apologised profusely. 'Come away inside for your tea, minister,' she advised, 'and don't bother your erse with them.'

THE MINISTER had been telling his Sunday School about the lost sheep and how Jesus had had ninety-nine of them, but had been distraught to have lost one and had been determined to find it.

'Now,' said the minister. 'It was very important to Jesus that he find the lost sheep, even although he had ninety-nine others. Does anybody know why?'

One wee lad from a nearby croft put up his hand and offered: 'It wid likely hae been the tup.'

A MINISTER in entirely another part of Aberdeenshire had been telling his Sunday School children about the importance of love against hate. 'Now,' he said, smiling, 'let's see if you can tell me the difference between love and hate. Can someone give me a sentence with the words Love and Hate in it?'

'Please, sir! Please, sir!'

'Yes, Willie, what's your sentence?'

'Please, sir! I love het pies!'

A VILLAGE worthy attending a funeral at Essil Church-yard, Garmouth, thanked the minister for the lovely address then, gathering himself up against the cold, sighed and said: 'Aye, I wid like fine to be beeried here in Essil. If I'm spared.'

ON A crowded railway carriage into Aberdeen in the late 1940s, a young minister was holding forth about how well he knew his Buchan parish. Somewhat ambitiously, he declared that he was sure he knew everything that was going on there.

An old chap leaned across and tapped him on the

knee. 'Excuse me, meenister,' he said. 'I ken something ee dinna ken.'

'Really?' said the minister.

'Aye. My wife's yer washerwumman, and I'm weerin een o' yer sarks.'

BEFORE THE war, in one particular North-east village was a garage staffed by a man called Bob who drove the village taxi and specialised in repairing bicycles. He also had an extremely pronounced stutter.

One night, the elderly village minister arrived with his equally elderly bike, wheeled it up beside the inspection pit and tapped Bob on the shoulder.

'Robert,' he said, 'would you have an old seat for my bicycle?'

Without turning round, Bob replied: 'Fit wye? Is the bu- bu- bugger ye've got nae aul enough?'

A RUNDOWN croft in the heart of Buchan was the home of Mrs Eppie McIntosh, her hens, her cows and her numerous cats who had the run of the house. Seeing the minister coming up the road towards the croft, presumably on his annual visit, she had just enough time to stuff the scattered papers and clothes under the cushions and rush to the door to greet him.

'Gweed morning, minister. Come awa in.'

Having settled himself in a chair by the fire, scattering cats in all directions, he was asked by Eppie if he would like a cup of tea. He had been warned by the kirk session of Eppie's standards of hygiene, but he accepted, albeit reluctantly.

Through to the kitchen she went and came back with a cup which was accepted graciously. Thinking that maybe it hadn't been near a sink for a wee while, the minister turned it deftly round to the other side and took a sip, only to hear Eppie remark:

'Aye, meenister, I see ye're left-handit lik masel.'

A VISITOR to the country met up with a farmer from the area round Mormond Hill and, in the course of the conversation, asked to which church he belonged.

'Oh,' said the farmer, 'that aa depens far the waddin or the funeral's bein held.'

A COUNTRY minister was taking a morning walk and came upon one of his Sunday School pupils feeding the farm poultry.

'Are all these hens yours, Willie?' he asked.

'Yes, sir,' said Willie.

Just then, the cock started crowing.

'Now, Willie,' said the minister, 'when the cock crows in the morning, do you know what that is invariably a sign of?'

'Yes, sir,' said Willie. 'It's a sign he's nae sleepin.'

IN THE days when there were no such things as linked charges, and every country church had a minister of its own, three of the most remote ministers turned up at the quarterly presbytery meeting, began chatting and discovered that all their churches had bats. They began swapping tips on how to contain the problem, and perhaps even get rid of them.

'I did suggest to a farmer nearby that he might be able to shoot at the creatures as they came out at night,' said the first minister, 'but I must confess it was not the most efficient solution, and I do feel a little guilty about it.'

'We strung a strawberry net over the hole under the eaves where they were nesting,' said the second. 'It worked up to a point, but there were still one or two who were able to wriggle free.'

The third minister put down his cup of tea. 'Jist baptise them,' he said. 'Ye'll nivver see them again.'

A RETIRED Donside minister who asks not to be named
says that he visited a sheltered-housing complex in 1992
to see one of his old parishioners, a spinster who had just
reached her 100th birthday.

The conversation wore round to marriage, and the
minister observed that she had never been courted or
betrothed. Had she never thought that the companionship
of wedlock would have been a comfort in her old age?

'Meenister,' she said, 'I'd a dog that snored, a lum that
smoked and a cat that wis oot a' nicht. Fit need hid I o'
a man?'

AFTER A wedding at Lumsden in the mid-1950s, the
minister was doing the social rounds of the guests and
came upon two Kildrummy worthies propping up the bar.
Both of them were known for long marriages. Sandy, in
fact, had celebrated his golden wedding not two weeks
before.

'Well, Sandy,' said the minister, 'another happy day, eh?
How does it make you feel seeing this young couple setting
out on the long path that you've travelled yourself these
last fifty years. They're in for a lot of happiness, eh?'

'Meenister,' said Sandy. 'Wullie and me here wis jist
sayin we didna ken fit happiness wis until we got mairriet.'

'Aye,' said Wullie. 'And then it wis ower late.'

THE SAME minister reports that later at the same wedding
reception he overheard Sandy and Wullie conversing with
another Kildrummy farmer, when Sandy turned to Wullie
and said: 'No, Sandy, like yersel, I couldna ask for a
better wife.'

Then he took another sip of his dram. 'I'd like til,' he
added, 'bit I widna dare.'

A MINISTER who preached once in the Church of Scotland in London in 1959 says that he noticed that there

were three pennies in the collection plate and joked from the pulpit: 'I see there are three pennies in the collection this morning. We must have an Aberdonian in our midst.'

'No,' said an English voice. 'Three of them.'

BILL DUGUID was travelling by train from Maud to Aberdeen in 1938 and found himself seated to what looked like a very stern-faced gentleman when a farmer in the seat opposite took out a bottle of whisky and began taking a swig.

The clergyman looked at the farmer disapprovingly. 'I'm sixty-five years old,' he said, 'and do you know I've never touched a drop of that awful stuff.'

'Aye, weel,' said the farmer, taking another swig. 'And ye winna be startin the day, eether.'

THE KIRK elders were not at all impressed with the sermon preached by the new minister, and said so to each other as they discussed it afterwards.

Opinions were many, but the general view was put most succinctly by the village grocer, who said: 'In the first place, he read it. In the second place, he didna read it weel. And in the third place, it wisna worth readin.'

Many a Good Tune

If some of the finest shafts of North-east wit come from old folk, that's probably because they have been steeped in it for far longer than the rest of us. We were sent more examples of senior-citizen humour than of any other category. The difficult decision was in choosing what to leave out.

BILL FROM Buckie was in his mid-70s when he suffered a massive heart attack while walking in the town square. He was rushed to the local hospital and from there by ambulance to Aberdeen Royal Infirmary.

The event was the speak of the Banffshire coast for some days until it became clear that Bill would pull through and would soon be back at his regular seat in his favourite bar.

On the day that he was due to be discharged from the ARI, a nursing sister visited him just to be sure that he was happy about the changes to his way of life that he would have to make. Bill nodded solemnly throughout the lecture.

'But I don't want to suggest that it's all gloom and doom,' she concluded. 'I mean, a lot of heart-attack patients go to ridiculous lengths to keep as inactive as possible. They wrap themselves in cotton wool, which is almost as bad as going out disco-dancing. You mustn't be scared of physical exertion just because of one heart attack. Nowadays, we think regular light exercise is possibly the best way to a speedy recovery.

'Heavens, there's no reason why you shouldn't resume sexual relations as soon as you get home.'

Bill looked at her. 'I'm sivventy-six,' he said. 'Wid it be OK if I hid a cup o' tea first?'

AN ELDERLY man from the heart of Aberdeenshire had

'Wid it be OK if I hid a cup o' tea first?'

decided to blow a substantial sum of money achieving his lifetime's ambition. He went on a Caribbean cruise and had a high old time, even although his thick country accent made communication difficult with a boatload of English, American, German, French and Canadian travellers.

At one port of call, many of the passengers were going ashore for a conducted tour when one man collapsed, unconscious, at the foot of the gangway. Heatstroke, was the verdict.

Our Aberdeenshire man, half-way back up the gangway, realised what was happening and was alarmed to see that the man had fallen very awkwardly, with one leg away to one side, his arms buckled under him and the other leg twisted to the left.

He knew enough about first aid to worry for the patient's comfort, and decided that the man had to be rearranged properly to make breathing easier. He had to be straightened out.

'Strachenimoot!' he cried. 'Strachenimoot!'

A ship's officer stopped him before he could reach the invalid. 'It's all right, sir,' he said. 'It's all right. Keep calm. We'll get you a German-speaking doctor.'

A TORPHINS woman was celebrating her 90th birthday but, unfortunately, had been bedridden and confused for several months. When her son and daughter-in-law visited to prepare her for a day of callers and wellwishers, they found her sitting up and looking immaculate. They reminded her that the new minister would be calling on her shortly.

A few moments later came a knock at the door and the doctor arrived for the old lady's weekly examination. The son let him into the house and the doctor showed himself into the bedroom.

After the doctor had examined her, he bade her good-day and left the room to explain to the son that the elderly lady was as well as could be expected. With the doctor gone, the son went in to see his mother and found her mildly upset.

'Fit's wrang, mither?' he inquired.

'He wis affa familiar for a minister,' she sniffed.

TWO WOMEN were in the queue at the Summerhill Post Office and were heard to be discussing their ailments. The larger one had clearly been to the doctor to see about a sore leg, and reported:

'He jist said that if it wis his leg, he widna worry aboot it.

'I jist telt him that if it wis his leg, I widna worry aboot it, eether.'

A RETIRED Garioch vet recalls attending a call to the home of a spinster at Inverurie who was celebrated for her devotion to her two cats. Apparently, one cat had been listless for a long time and was now miaowing and in great pain.

Almost as soon as the vet clapped eyes on the cat, he realised that the animal was heavily pregnant and told the old woman as much.

She was aghast.

'Oh, bit foo could that hiv happened?' she said. 'I dinna let her oot o' the hoose, for I'm feart for exactly that kinna thing.'

The vet looked across at a big tomcat filling an armchair on the other side of the living-room.

'What about him?' he suggested.

'Och, nivver,' said the woman. 'That's her brither.'

AN ELDERLY gentleman turned up at a travel agency at Peterhead and seemed reluctant to seek advice, but stood poring over racks of brochures against the wall. Eventually, an assistant went across to see if she could help.

'Aye, lassie, I wis jist winderin if ye dee holidays in Scotland.'

'Yes, we do,' she said. 'Come and take a seat.'

While the old chap seated himself, the assistant gathered together a pile of brochures and spread them on the counter before him. 'Were you thinking of anywhere in particular?'

'I'd a notion for a wikkend at Dunbar.'

'A very nice place. Would you be going yourself?'

'Na, na, I'd better tak the wife wi me, seein as it's wir ruby anniversary.'

'Oh, a celebration, that's marvellous. Does she know or is it a secret?'

'No, she disna ken yet.'

'Oh, super. She'll get a real surprise.'

'She will that. She's expectin a fortnicht in Tenerife.'

A BLIZZARD was blowing up the Cabrach and the scatter of crofters were becoming increasingly worried about Dod, who stayed by himself and whose but and ben at the heid o' the glen was prone to being covered by drifts.

A concerned group gathered and set off to be sure that Dod was all right. They struggled on foot up the glen to where they thought the house would be, but there was no sign. They began probing the drifts with the long sticks they had brought and, eventually, one of them hit the corrugated-iron roof. After a few moments digging, they cleared the lum.

'Are ye a'richt, Dod?' shouted one man down the lum above the raging storm.

'Deein gran,' came a faint voice from inside. 'I'm cosied up and I've plenty o' a'thing.'

'We wis thinkin we'd dig ye oot,' shouted the neighbour. 'It's a hell o' a nicht oot here. The sna's blaain lik the verra deevil. We'll be as quick's we can. Can ye wyte or we dig ye oot?'

'Dig me oot?!' came the indignant reply. 'Fit the hell wid I dee oot on a nicht lik this?'

BETWEEN THE wars, Maggie and Tam lived on Deeside and, once a month in the summer, Maggie demanded that Tam yoke the pony and trap and drive her for the day to visit her numerous relatives in Buchan. Bored to tears, Tam passed the days sauntering through the unfamiliar villages.

'Fit kinna placie wis it that ye visited yestreen?' inquired one of Tam's friends the following day.

'Nae worth a damn,' said Tam. 'Nae even a decent war memorial ti read.'

WILLIE LIVED a very spartan life near Keith in a ramshackle but and ben at the back of beyond. His dog was his companion, with two hens that used to lay his breakfast eggs every morning, but his diet consisted of tins of this and tins of that.

After one kind lady's Christmas lunch, she packed her family's leftovers and trudged four miles through the snow to Willie's cottage. His face was a picture when he saw the spread being laid before him, but he still gave her a stern telling off for venturing so far in the snow.

And Willie had a substantial repast, with a paper tablecloth over the wooden teachest which served as his table, then Christmas cracker, dram, soup, turkey and trimmings, trifle, Christmas pudding with brandy and a cup of tea. She had brought candles, as she knew Willie's old Tilley lamp was unreliable; bones for the dog and crumbs for the hens.

After everything had been done to perfection, she decided she had better get home, as the snow was falling more heavily. She left, telling Willie that she would return in a few days to pick up her containers and dishes once the roads were cleared and the snow melted.

Two weeks later, she ventured back and Willie was sitting at the fireside, puffing on his pipe. Words were scarce and she suspected that something was amiss.

'Foo are ye, Wullie?'

'A'richt, I suppose.'

She collected all her containers and dishes and, after half an hour, when still no reference had been made to the meal, she inquired gently: 'Did you enjoy the Christmas dinner I gave you?'

'I did,' he said, 'bit ye'd ower muckle saat in yer gravy.'

GERTIE LOST her teeth after the war and never bothered to replace them. She was happy with her lot and never minded that she was gumsie. Her neighbour, however, was embarrassed about it and invited Gertie over for an afternoon fly cup.

Gertie was a little suspicious, especially since the neighbour was not in the habit of inviting the lower orders in for afternoon tea. However, she knew that the woman's father had not long died, and decided she should at least call to pay her respects to the family.

'Now Gertie,' said the neighbour, sitting her down on the settee, 'I've kent ye a lang time, and I've a proposition for ye.'

'Fit wid that be?'

The neighbour produced a fancy box and pressed it into Gertie's hands. 'Here ye are,' she said, 'as ye ken, ma faither is nae lang deed, and his teeth were barely twa month aul. There wis nae pint beeryin him wi a dear set o' teeth, so I jist said til ma man that we'd gie Gertie first refusal.'

ONE DISTRICT nurse wrote to tell us of old Jock, who kept a rusty chuntie (chamberpot) on the sideboard with a beautiful show of lillies growing out of it.

'What a bonnie show o' lillies ye hiv, Jock,' she said, and she ventured closer for a sniff, only to discover to her horror that the compost was somewhat pungent, to say the least. In fact, it overcame the scent of the lillies.

'Weel, quine,' said Jock, noticing her distress. 'The secret's a kniv-fae o' dung stappit weel doon, bit ye're likely smellin the twa mothballs at the boddim.'

A QUEUE had developed at the chemist's and people became most alarmed when an ill-natered old-timer got to the front and demanded 'a tube o' Semtex'.

The pharmacist suggested that he must have got it wrong. Semtex was a highly unstable explosive much favoured by terrorists. What did he want it for?

'I've a sair-blockit nose and I'm needin it unblockit.'

'Ah,' said the chemist, the mists clearing. 'You mean Sinex.'

A RETIRED farmer was walking through woods near Cults on a Sunday constitutional when a wood pigeon spotted him and covered the lapels of the old chap's brand-new Sunday suit liberally with droppings.

The man's wife, who was strolling with him and who wrote to us, said she had a hard time keeping a straight face when her husband looked disapprovingly at the clartit lapel, then looked up at where the bird was still sitting on the branch of a tree and said simply:

'Min, fit wis the eese o' that?'

TWO WOMEN – one as big and bosomy as the other was small and mousy – were standing at an Inverurie bus shelter on a wintry day when slush lay in the gutter and icy winds whipped down West High Street. Our confidant doesn't know how the conversation began, because he joined the queue behind them half-way through, but he jaloused quickly that it concerned a bus running over and killing a small girl's pet dog.

'Of coorse, the bus driver wis affa sorry,' said Bella.

'Affa sorry,' repeated Violet, hanging intently on her companion's tale.

'He couldna stop, ye see. He said there wid hiv been an accident if he'd stoppit. The doggie jist ran oot in front o' him. Even the bobby could see that.'

'Even the bobby,' repeated Violet.

'Of coorse, the quinie wis jist brakkin her hert. Brakkin her hert, the quinie. She couldna hiv been mair nor eicht. And what sorry I felt for her. It wis her doggie, ye see. She wis sobbin. I wis sniffin. Michty, the bus driver wis near greetin, tee. It wis jist tragic.'

'Jist tragic.'

At that, the bus hove in sight. Bella peered at a handful of small change and strode out over the slush and into the roadside. 'Aye, weel,' she said, 'a bonnie little doggie it micht hiv been, bit it's flat as a kipper noo.'

THE WHITE Settler phenomenon – people arriving from outwith the North-east and installing themselves on all sorts of committees within five minutes to run organisations in communities about which they know comparatively nothing – is not new. Many years ago, a Cockney family arrived in Lower Deeside.

One evening, the mother and daughter of the new family decided it would be nice to get to know the neighbours and paid a visit to the neighbouring farm at Newton.

The tenant farmer of the Newton put up with the conversation for some time, but the two visitors were terrible blethers and, anyway, he had great difficulty in understanding the Cockney tongue.

Eventually, impatience got the better of him and he stormed out with: 'Gweed sakes, wummen, will ye haud yer tongues an lat fowk that can spikk, spikk.'

ERNIE, FROM Stonehaven, was proud that he had kept himself in much the same physical condition that he had enjoyed during his Army days, when he had been a physical-training instructor with the Desert Rats. He prided himself on his good health, youthful looks and general trimness.

While on a visit to Aberdeen, he spotted that one of the cinemas had a special deal on for matinee showings, offering cut rates for pensioners. He decided he would take his wife to see a weepie, just as they had in their courting days.

He told the assistant in the ticket booth how old he was and said he would easily show her his bus pass if she needed more proof.

'No, it disna maitter,' said the young girl, 'I can see yer face.'

BILL HENDERSON, an Aberdeen-based financial adviser, told us of visiting a 93-year-old man at Inverurie to go over his investments. The old chap listened carefully as Bill ran through everything in fine detail and eventually pronounced himself happy. Ever the salesman, Bill tried to introduce him to a new five-year bond.

The old boy listened patiently while Bill ran through the sales pitch, then he leaned forward and said quietly: 'I dinna think so, Mr Henderson. At my age, I dinna even buy green bananas.'

Mixter Maxter

On the grounds that every decent filing system has to have a Miscellaneous section, we're not going to disappoint anyone. Here are the tales that did not fit easily in one of the other chapters. Look on it as the Lucky Dip you enjoyed so much at the agricultural shows of your childhood.

IN THE mid-1960s, it was not uncommon for small travelling circuses to set up their marquees in showparks even at small North-east villages. On two summer evenings in 1964, the Showpark at Alford was host to one such circus and most of the village young fry and their parents turned out to attend.

At one point came the obligatory spectacle of sawing a woman in half, and the ringmaster announced that the swarthy young man performing the trick had been perfecting his art for more than 15 years, for it had been his ambition ever since he had been a small boy.

Jimmy Harper, sitting in the audience with two of his four daughters, turned to the man sitting next to him and said: 'That'll be the laddie wi fower half-brithers.'

IT IS said that one elderly member of the aristocracy, whose seat was in Aberdeenshire, had been attending the village show one summer in the 1930s when he had approached the 'Penny A Kiss' stand, behind which stood a pretty young lass of about 16. His lordship, who had an eye for the ladies and a wicked sense of humour, approached the stand, fumbled in his waistcoat pocket for sixpence, and presented to the girl, then puckered his wizened lips.

With great presence of mind, the girl turned to an elderly woman in her sixties next to her and said: 'Grandma, maybe you could attend til Lord ——?'

His Lordship opened his eyes and then, quite unruffled,

turned to his manservant and said: 'Please attend to this purchase.' And walked off.

ANDREW CRUICKSHANK, the Aberdeen-born actor who went on to play Dr Cameron in the BBC TV version of Doctor Finlay, used to tell a story of attending Aikey Fair as a small boy and being mesmerised by a stall set up by a quack doctor.

The quack was peddling a muddy-brown liquid in small bottles, and hoardings to left and right proclaimed the liquid as a cure for what seemed, to the young Cruickshank, like every ailment and affliction known to man.

'Roll up! Roll up!' shouted the quack 'This miracle liquid will cure every ache, pain and disease known to medical science. It will even cure old age.'

When the crowd began to look sceptical, he announced, with barely a hint of a smile: 'If you don't believe me, I can reveal that I am more than a hundred and twenty years old.'

The crowd's scepticism grew even louder, until one woman looked at the teenage girl taking the cash behind a table stacked with the bottles and demanded: 'Is 'at true?'

'Don't ask me,' said the girl. 'I've only been working with him for sixty-two years.'

AN ESTATE agent was showing a young professional English couple round a country cottage not a stone's throw from the knackery near Kintore. Clearly, the knackery had been busy and, to make matters worse, a nearby farmer was muckspreading.

The couple stood it for 20 minutes until they could stand it no longer. 'Frankly,' said the husband, 'I'm a little surprised you bothered to show us here. Is it always like this?'

'Nae aye,' said the estate agent. Then, realising he had probably lost the sale, added: 'But think on the advantages.'

'What advantages?'

'Ye aye ken fitna wye the win's blawin.'

ONE RETIRED Inverurie woman teacher reports taking a long-weekend cruise to Shetland with a female friend. The North Sea can be incredibly rough and, on this occasion, lived up to its reputation; barely anyone aboard escaped sickness.

'Don't worry,' said the teacher to her green-faced companion, 'nobody's ever died of a wee bit of seasickness.'

'Oh,' groaned the woman, 'what a peety. It's only the thocht o' death that's keepin me alive.'

THE CLERK of works at a North-east town council (who is still alive, so no names) had an office worker who would nip out in the middle of every morning for a swig from a bottle of whisky he kept in the basket of his bike. He would also eat a peppermint to try to hide the smell.

One morning, one of the office-worker's colleagues went out early and swopped the bag of peppermints for a jar of pickled onions. At 10.30, the man duly had his swig of whisky and was aghast to find no peppermints. With no option, he bit into a pickled onion.

A few moments after his return, the clerk of works called him across. 'How long have you worked here?'

'Six years.'

'Exactly. Six years I've put up with whisky and peppermint, but if it's going to be whisky and pickled onion you'll need to find another job.'

IN THE days when Keith was a busy railway junction, one of the platforms was notoriously high and open, and one visitor, accompanied by a Keith woman and being seen away after a holiday, commented on the potential dangers to one of the station staff.

'Ye aye ken fitna wye the win's blawin.'

'It's a wonder there isn't a warning sign,' she said.

'There wis a sign,' said the railman. 'Bit naebody at Keith's as stupid as they wid fa aff a platform, so we took it doon.'

A MEMBER of a Central Belt Rotary Club wrote to tell us about attending a national convention in 1988 and meeting a delegate from the North-east. One evening, they fell to talking about life, love and families and the man from the Central Belt took a picture from his wallet and showed him three boys, pink, scrubbed and smiling.

The man from the North-east took the picture and studied it, smiling. 'That's a nice photie,' he said. 'I wish I hid three loons.'

'Have you not got any family, then?' said the Glasgow man, taking the picture back.

'Aye,' said the North-east man. 'Five quines.'

DEESIDE BETWEEN the wars was known for its Royal connections, but it could claim fame also at the other end of the social spectrum; communities everywhere from Banchory to Braemar were favoured spots for Scotland's tinkers and travelling families each summer.

One tinker was supposedly stopped on the road one evening by a solitary figure, who had obviously been out shooting, and was asked for a match.

Someone who witnessed the incident informed the tinker later that he had had the privilege of being in the presence of the Duke of York.

Shortly afterwards, tinker and 'sportsman' met again. Once again, the sportsman was without a match.

On being asked, the tinker once again produced a match but, as he handed it over, remarked: 'It's a terrible thing that a man lik me is supposed ti keep the king's bairn in spunks.'

THE SCENE is a roup (auction sale) at a craftie at Rora. Sandy Bell is auctioneer and George Mackie is showing the goods. 'Right,' says Sandy, as George holds up a double-burner glass lamp, three-quarters full of paraffin, 'fit for this lump, noo?'

There is some mildly animated conversation, but no concrete interest.

'Come on, noo,' says Sandy, 'there's aboot a gallon o' paraffin in't.'

'Aye,' shouts Willie Duncan from the floor, 'and aboot a fortnicht o' wikk.'

SANDY WAS forever fa'in doon throwe his English. One evening, while about to start compering the local-hall concert, he announced:

'We're affa sorry, bit Mrs Soutar canna be wi's the nicht ti play the pianna. She's decomposed. Hooivver, Mrs Mack, the doctor's wife, his agreed ti be the prostitute and, as a'body here kens, she'll dee a gran job o't.'

FORMER PAGE Three girl Linda Lusardi was invited one year to open the Oldmeldrum Sports, a considerably brave departure from the normal roll of celebrities invited to do duty.

'Fa's this openin the show?' one worthy was heard to ask his companion.

'That's that deem that taks aff her claes in the papers,' said the other.

The two of them studied the ample Miss Lusardi for a few moments as she walked round the ring, then the first turned to the second:

'A gey change fae Maitland Mackie, onywye.'

A TAXI firm in the glens of West Aberdeenshire was asked for a good, safe driver for a wedding, and he had to be a teetotaller so that the bride's parents could be sure that their daughter's day wouldn't be spoiled.

'Canna help ye there,' said the boss. 'We hinna onybody lik that, bit I can gie ye a driver that ye'll nivver fill fu.'

THE REASON Aberdonians like golf, Edwin Reid informs us, is that the better they get the less wear there is on the clubs.

THE SCENE is Briggies, the local name for the Allargue Arms at Cockbridge, and mine host Airchie is sweelin the glasses waiting for the men of the Lonach Pipe Band to return from their outing to the Nethybridge Games. The last of the tourists have bedded down and suddenly, on the stroke of midnight, the Lonach Men explode on the place to tell of the success or otherwise of the piping competition across the hills.

As if to prove the exercise, out come the pipes, drums, busbys and all and soon the bar is filled with music and marching – a dirl enough to wake the dead.

It certainly stirs one couple whose bedroom is right above the action. They uptail and slink off into the night without so much as a goodbye.

Three weeks later, one of the pipers asked Airchie: 'A'thing a'richt, Airchie?'

'Michty aye,' said Airchie. 'A couple walkit oot athoot peyin on the nicht o' the Nethybrig Games, bit I got the best o' them; he left his pyjamas ahin, and I've been weerin them ivver since.'

THE LONACH is celebrated as one of the most historic community events in Scotland, drawing an audience from around the world. Its traditions are many and various, but the most notable is the march of the Men of Lonach, when 130 kilted hielanders tramp seven miles of Strathdon, stopping off along the route to partake of drams provided by hosts of castle and ha'.

Dr Innes, a son of the schoolhouse, was actually domiciled in Humberside, but dutifully travelled north on the appropriate August Saturday to be sure that tradition was upheld.

'Tell me, Dr Innes,' one of his Yorkshire colleagues asked him one year, 'what is it that takes you north at the end of August every year?'

'Ah, my freen,' he said. 'It is my most pleasant duty to dispense one hundred and thirty drams to the Men of Lonach on their march.

'And then I spend the rest of the day trying to avoid one hundred and thirty thirsty highlanders determined to stand their hand back to me.'

NOT OFTEN is the Lonach spoiled by bad weather, but when the heavens do open stories abound of previous experiences in the rain. Willie Gray, the bard o' Briggies, regaled those within earshot as to how rain seldom stopped work on farms. He took his fellow-clansmen back to the days when steam-driven threshing engines powered the threshing mills on visits to farms at the tail end of the hairst.

'Aye,' said Willie, 'I mind ae eer fin the hivvens open't and the rain nivver deval't. We stoppit in the efterneen for wir fly-cup and nivver got yokit again.'

'Oh?' said an attentive clansman next to him. 'Wis it ower coorse ti yoke?'

'Na,' said Willie. 'Ma cup widna teem.'

WHEN YOUR co-author (the one that presents radio programmes) visited the Edinburgh studios of BBC Radio Scotland to record a dance-music programme, he went into the reception area to ask if he could use the phone to contact home.

Mission accomplished, the receptionist asked him: 'Tell

me, are there words that cannot be translated from the English into the Gaelic?'

'Oh, aye,' he said. 'Wirds lik television, ile rigs, helicopters and the like, I wid imagine.' Then he thought for a moment. 'By the by, fit wye are ye askin me? I dinna hae the Gaelic.'

'Oh,' said the receptionist, 'so what was that you were speaking on the phone to your wife?'

And they say the Doric is not a language.

THE DAYS of the travelling dramatic societies in the North-east are sadly over. The favourite plays were in the Doric, of course, and included such as Mains Wooin and The Wee Reid Lums.

Abbie Moir had been a leading light with his Culter group over many years and recalled a visit to the Powis School Theatre in Aberdeen, where they were staging The Red Barn Mystery. Abbie, as William, had gently persuaded Maria out to the barn. The sound and lighting effects denoted a terrible night of thunder and lightning, and heightened the suspense, as the audience was aware that William had murder in mind.

The villain was down on his knees with his hands round Maria's neck. Abbie's acting must have been powerful and compelling, indeed, for one lad up in the balcony, for he jumped up, unable to contain his temper any longer, and shouted:

'Let er go, ye bugger! Ye're chokin er!'

UNTIL THE early 1980s, Aberdeen cars had the registration letters RS and RG, while Aberdeenshire had AV and SA. Naturally, the registration autorities had to be careful of any offensive combinations of letters, which was why the registration LAV was never issued. They also decreed that ARS should never be issued, which shows presumably that the diktat came from Down South.

They were certainly quite unaware of the local pronunciation, because they permitted (and still do) ERS.

ALL NORTH-EAST villages are fuelled on gossip. In many cases, what is not known is made up or embellished into a decent scandal out of all proportion to the truth. There are many stories, but the most succinct came from a native of Rhynie, describing her village.

Both of us would like to stress to Rhynie residents that we have nothing against Rhynie, and that this came from one of your own.

'If ye fart at the tap eyn o' Rhynie, it's intil a heap o' dirt by the time it's oot at the fit.'

A MEMBER of the check-in staff at Aberdeen Airport was said to have been treated to disciplinary action after he hung a piece of mistletoe over the check-in desk. When departing passengers asked what the mistletoe was there for, he would tell them: 'So you can kiss your luggage goodbye.'

BILL WAS a fiddler who owed more to enthusiasm than expertise, but still he persisted in entertaining at concert parties. In the early 1960s, he established himself down the bill in a short variety season at the Tivoli Theatre, Aberdeen, largely by diversifying into comedy, at which he was considerably better than the fiddle-playing.

One evening, he arrived later than usual for his call, and a new stage-door hand stopped him, pointed at the violin case and asked what was inside.

Bill was indignant. 'It's a machine-gun,' he said.

'Thank hivven for that,' said the young lad. 'I wis feart it wis yer fiddle.'

JIM LAWRIE was a doyen of Aberdeen hotel porters in the early 1970s, and did duty at several city hotels, but the famous story about Jim concerns the time he showed an important American gent up to his room.

The American was one of the most awkward customers Jim had encountered, putting him to all sorts of needless trouble, changing his mind about the order in which his cases had to be brought up, and so on. To cap it all, he didn't even offer a tip.

Half an hour later, the American called down to reception and asked for the bellboy to be sent up. Jim duly appeared at the door.

'Say, maybe you could come in and show me where the air-conditioning controls are,' drawled the Yank.

'There's nae air-conditionin in this hotel, sir,' said Jim drily.

'No air-conditioning?' gasped the Yank. 'Ya hear that, honey, there ain't no air-conditioning in this hotel. Tell me, boy, what am I supposed to do if it gets too hot or too cold?'

'Weel,' sighed Jim. 'I suggest ye open a windae or fart.'

The Ones That Got Away

We're certainly not suggesting that the people who sent us these tales were passing them off as the genuine article when they owe more to myth and fancy, but let's say both of us had heard variations on these themes over the years and we didn't want to risk the truth of the rest of the book by including them among the others. Still, some of them were too good to waste so, with a warning that you enter this chapter at your own risk, feel free.

KEEPING A nationally-renowned pipe band going is a costly business and needs a good deal of investment and fundraising. The story goes that the Oldmeldrum and District Pipe Band decided on a door-to-door collection, and each band member was dispatched to one particular part of town.

One came to a neatly kept pensioner's house and knocked on the door. An old body came and asked what he wanted.

'I'm collectin for the Oldmeldrum and District Pipe Band,' he said.

She cupped her hand to her ear. 'I'm a bittie deif,' she said. 'Ye maun spik up.'

'I'm collectin for the Oldmeldrum and District Pipe Band,' he said a little more loudly.

She screwed up her face in puzzlement. 'Na,' she said. 'Canna mak ye oot ata. Fit is it ye're sikkin?'

'*I'm collectin for the Oldmeldrum and District Pipe Band!*' he shouted.

She shook her head again and, realising he was working against impossible odds, he shook his head, gave her a weary wave and turned and walked back down the path. He clattered the gate shut behind him.

'Watch ma gate!' she shouted angrily.

'Ach, bugger yer gate,' he said.

'Aye,' she said. 'And bugger yer Oldmeldrum and District Pipe Band.'

THE MOTHER of a kitchie-deem at a big country house in Formartine marched up to the door and demanded to see the laird.

'It's oor Nellie,' she said. 'We think she's pregnant wi a' yer capers and we'd like ti ken fit ye intend deein aboot it.'

The laird looked flummoxed for a moment then said: 'All right. All right. If she really is pregnant, I'll give her ten thousand pounds and put another twenty thousand in trust for the baby. Will that keep it quiet?'

The woman had the wind taken from her sails, but recovered enough composure to say: 'Fairly that. And if she's nae pregnant, will ye gie her anither chunce?'

AN ABOYNE man went in for his morning paper, whistling. The newsagent was struck by how cheery the customer was, and said so. 'Aye,' agreed the man. 'It's ma birthday the day.'

'Well, congratulations,' said the newsagent. 'How old are you?'

'Foo aul d'ye think I am?'

'Fifty?'

'Na, I'm jist forty.'

The man went along to the baker, for his morning butteries, still whistling.

'Ye're real happy the day,' said the baker.

'Ma birthday,' explained the man.

'Congratulations,' said the baker. 'Foo aul are ye?'

'Foo aul d'ye think I am?'

'Fifty?'

'Na, I'm jist forty.'

The man went along to the grocer, for his pint of milk, still whistling.

'We think she's pregnant wi a' yer capers.'

'Ye're real happy the day,' said the grocer.

'Ma birthday,' explained the man.

'Congratulations,' said the grocer. 'Foo aul are ye?'

'Foo aul d'ye think I am?'

'Fifty?'

'Na, I'm jist forty.'

The man went out to the bus stop, still whistling and stood behind a woman in her eighties, waiting for the bus to Ballater.

'Michty,' she said. 'Somebody's affa cheery the day.'

'Ma birthday,' explained the man.

'Congratulations,' said the old woman. 'Foo aul are ye?'

'Foo aul d'ye think I am?'

She studied him up and down. 'Well,' she said warily, 'I widna like ti say, bit I ken a foolproof wye that I can tell.'

'And fit's that?'

'If I gie ye a richt slubbery kiss and then rub yer backside.'

The man was a little taken aback, but looked at the little old lady and thought there was no harm in it, so he bent forward to receive a wet slubbery kiss and then stuck out his behind so she could give it a good stroke.

'Now,' he said. 'Foo aul am I?'

'Ye're forty.'

He was amazed. 'Foo on earth did ye ken that?'

'I wis stannin ahen ye in the queue at the baker's.'

WE WON'T trouble you with the famous-but-hoary old 'Aa ae oo?' story, but we liked the tale of the country loon visiting the Lecht ski slope for the first time, struggling to put on his skis and looking up plaintively to ask:

'Fit fit fits fit fit?'

THEY SAY that a farmer visited the Smithfield Show for the first time late in his career and was amazed by the sights and sounds of the Big Smoke. He decided to stay on for an extra day just to savour London life.

All was going well until his braces snapped, perhaps with the exertions of climbing up and down the steps into the Underground. He nipped into a post office just off Regent Street.

'I'll tak a pair o' yer galluses, ma dear,' he informed the woman behind the glass once he got to the head of the queue.

'I beg your pardon?'

'A pair o' galluses, ma dear. I'll tak a pair o' galluses.'

'Galluses?'

'Galluses. Ye ken. Braces. For haudin up yer brikks.'

'Braces? I'm sorry, sir. This is a post office.'

'I ken that fine.'

'But we don't sell braces in a post office.'

'Well, they div at Auchnagatt.'

A YOUNG mother from Fraserburgh was becoming increasingly fed up with her brood's incessant demands for sweeties. On one shopping trip to Aberdeen, her patience finally snapped. 'Lord,' she shouted. 'If ye dinna stop aetin a' that gulshach, ye'll be that fat that folk'll aye be lookin at ye.'

On their way home on the bus, the boy noticed a very pretty, but heavily pregnant, young woman getting on, and he began smiling to himself. Not many miles along the road, she caught his gaze and he smiled at her. She smiled back and his smile broadened into a grin and a steady stare.

Eventually, she became puzzled and leaned across to him. 'Div I ken you, or div you ken me?'

'I dinna ken ye,' said the boy, 'bit I ken fit ye've been deein.'

A MACDUFF skipper put to sea and after a few hours decided to grab a bit of sleep and instructed the youngest and greenest member of the crew to keep watch and report if he spotted anything that he thought the skipper should know about.

The lad scanned the horizon intently and eventually, just after the skipper had nodded off, burst in on him and said: 'Skipper! Skipper! There's a seagull!'

'For ony sake, laddie!' stormed the skipper. 'Ye wakken me up ti tell me that! I telt ye that ye should only disturb me if it wis something that wid interest me! And ye wakken me for a bliddy seagull!'

'Oh, bit I think ye'll be interestit in this seagull, skipper. It's sittin on a rock.'

TWO FARMERS boarded the train at Torphins and were sitting smoking their pipes in silence when a commercial traveller entered.

'Good morning, gentlemen,' he said brightly. He was met with glares and silence.

The traveller left the carriage at Banchory and bade the farmers farewell with: 'Good day, Gentlemen. A very pleasant day to you both.'

One farmer looked at the other, took the pipe from his mouth and said: 'A gabbin vratch.'

THE MAN from Littlewoods called to tell the Donside farmworker that he had won almost £1 million on the pools. The man was shocked and delighted all at once, and invited the Littlewoods representative inside, apologising for the state of the house, but his wife was away visiting her parents for a few days.

They went through the paperwork, then the Littlewoods man asked him how he thought he'd spend the money.

'Oh,' said the farmworker, 'This his a' happened real sudden. I hinna hid time ti think. I suppose I'll likely hae a holiday. A new car. Maybe I'll buy masel a new hoose. See ma relations in Australia. A cruise, maybe.'

'And what about your wife?' said the Littlewoods man. 'What will she be buying herself?'

'Lord,' said the farmworker, 'dinna tell me she's won the pools, as weel.'

ANOTHER POOLS winner – this time a Buchan farmer – was asked how he would spend his windfall. Would he buy a fancy car? A villa in Portugal? Go on a world cruise? Or just retire?

'Na, na,' he said. 'I'll jist fairm awa til the money gings deen.'

WHAT'S THE difference between stubborn and that good Doric word thrawn? The dictionary will tell you that there is no difference; that thrawn is merely another word for stubborn (a N. Brit. Dial. word, to be precise).

But there's a big difference between stubborn and thrawn, as the following apocryphal story shows. An illness had threatened to disrupt the activities of a Formartine primary school. Two boys had very sore tummies, which the school nurse put down to constipation. Both were sent home with wee notes of the ailment and the suggested remedy.

Mother No. 1 read the note and went for a bottle of syrup of figs from the chemist. 'Noo, Johnnie,' she said. 'The nursie says ye maun tak yer syrup o' figs for yer constipation.'

'I will not.'

'Ye will sut.'

'Winna.'

And so the battle commenced with no suitable outcome. That's stubborn.

Over at Mother No. 2's: 'Noo, Billy, the nursie says ye maun tak yer syrup o' figs for yer constipation.'

'I will not.'

'Ye will sut.'

'Winna.'

And so a ding-dong battle ensued, much as before, except that in this case, Billy was worn down eventually by sheer fatigue and, to get the matter over and done with, relented slightly.

'OK,' he said. 'I'll tak the syrup o' figs.'

His mother duly administered it.

With a furious scowl on his face, half born of rage and half of the dreadful taste of the medicine, Billy stormed off, saying: 'A'richt. I've taen it noo. I've taen the bliddy syrup o' figs.

'Bit I winna poop.'

And that's thrawn.

THERE IS nothing more enjoyable than a country wedding reception in a village hall. North-east folk seem to be more at home there than at a posh hotel, yet the food, the decoration and the formal proceedings are the same.

At a wedding a few years back up Deeside, the main guests were seated at the top table, including the minister beside the bride's mother and the bride's father seated next to the groom's mother, and so on, and so on. The usual set-oot.

Along came a waiter with the drinks and he asked the bride's father if he would care for a whisky.

'Michty aye. Fairly, fairly,' said the father, and a dram was duly set down in front of him.

The waiter moved along the top table and, coming to the minister, asked if he, too, would like a dram.

'Do you not see I'm a man of the cloth?' said the minister. 'And you offer me whisky? How disgusting. How inappropriate. I would rather commit adultery.'

At which the bride's father handed back his glass, saying: 'Michty, I didna ken we'd a choice.'

THE YEAR that Aberdeen's seagull population exploded was certainly 1995, when glorious weather brought a most unwelcome problem to The Toon – fouling, scavenging and din throughout the city. The letters columns in the newspapers were full of debate for weeks.

Two lads of simple mind were having a walk around the Harbour when a seagull spotted one of them well and truly, and scored a direct hit, all over the lad's head and shoulders.

'God dammit,' he said. 'Look at me noo. Hiv ye bit paper, Sandy?'

'That winna dee ony good,' said Sandy. 'The damnt bird's miles awa or noo.'

TWO SONS of New Deer, who had left for work in London and had retired there, had been unable to make it home for the funeral of one of their former cronies who had died, but they turned up together the following summer, by which time the headstone was in place, but it had subsided badly and was leaning at a jaunty angle.

Davie found a piece of wire at the gravedigger's bothy and managed a makeshift repair by tying the wire securely to the headstone and tying the other end to a nearby fencepost. He intended going round to see the widow and explaining that maybe someone had better try a more permanent repair.

The two of them were just about to leave the cemetery, when two of the village's older ladies walked past the stone and stopped to look.

'Wid ye credit that?' said one to the other. 'Geordie dee't nae sax month syne, and he's got the phone in already.'

GIBBY AND Erchie had gone on a package holiday to Rome with their wives. One evening, while the girls went sightseeing, the lads repaired to a bar and asked the barman for a sample of the local brew.

'What about this?' said the barman, showing them a bottle of creme de menthe. 'This is what the Pope drinks.'

'If it's gweed enough for His Popeness, it's gweed enough for us,' said Gibby. 'Gies twa pints o' yer creme de menthe.'

The barman obliged and watched them, amused, as they struggled through the creme de menthe and were soon near unconscious. The next thing they knew, it was six in the morning and they were streaked out on the floor of a bus shelter in a Rome suburb, both with splitting headaches, dry mouths and shaking limbs.

'Michty,' said Gibby, trying in vain to haul himself upright. 'If that's fit the Pope drinks it's nae muckle winner he gets aff planes and fa's on his knees.'

A WIDOW was being comforted on the night before the funeral by her daughter and two of her closest neighbours. One of the neighbours remarked that the widow seemed to be remarkably composed, and hoped that the grief wouldn't hit when all the friends and family had departed and suddenly she realised she was on her own.

'No,' said the widow, looking at her husband in his coffin. 'I'll be fine. Geordie spent a' wir mairriet life oot drinkin and bowlin and gamblin and playin aboot wi ither weemin. This is the first nicht in years I've kent far he is.'

MYSIE AND Dod from Strathbogie had been trying for almost 10 years to start a family when, one day, Mysie decided she had better go for a pregnancy test. Later, the doctor studied the results, then leaned across the consulting desk and patted her hand.

'Well, Mysie,' he said, 'I'm delighted to tell you that after all these years, you're expecting.'

Mysie was overcome, almost on the point of tears with relief and happiness. 'Oh, doctor,' she said, her voice quavering, 'that's the best news we could hiv hopit for.

I winder if I could hae a shottie o' yer phone so I could phone Dod at his work.'

The doctor smiled and pushed the phone towards her. She dialled the number, waited a few moments and asked to be put through to Dod at his desk.

'Oh, Dod, Dod,' she said. 'I've got news for ye. I'm pregnant!'

There was a deep silence at the other end, followed by a cautious: 'Fa's spikkin?'

BERTIE WAS one of those townspeople before the war who were celebrated for their slow wit, but who were never really as slow as townsfolk liked to think. Bertie's stance was on the Plainstones at Banff, where he would lean and watch the world go by, and most of the townspeople would give him a cheery wave as they went about their business.

It was a favourite sport of the more exalted townsfolk from the southern end of town to go for a Sunday stroll, see Bertie in his usual spot on the Plainstones, and go up to try a little test to amuse their wives. A man would hold out a shilling in one hand and a threepenny bit in the other and tell Bertie he could have his pick to keep.

Bertie always chose the 3d.

When a nearby shopkeeper could bear the insult to Bert no longer, she bustled out of her shop the following morning and said: 'Bertie, surely ye ken that the nobs are jist takkin ye for a feel. I saw them yestreen, jist like I've seen them ilky Sunday. They offer ye a shillin and a thripny and they think it's great fun fin ye jist tak the thripny. Fit wye div ye nae tak the shillin? It's worth four times as muckle.'

'I ken that, mistress,' said Bertie. 'I ken that fine. Bit if I took the shillin, they widna come back the next Sunday.'

CHARLIE AND Mary were out for a Sunday runnie in their new Austin one day when a police patrol car pulled out of a hiding place at the end of a farm road and began following them. Sure enough, a few miles later the blue lights went on and Charlie drew into the side.

The bobby strolled up and tapped on the window, and Charlie rolled it down.

'Fit's yer hurry?' said the bobby. 'This is a forty-mile-an-oor area. Ye were deein at least sixty.'

'I wis jist deein forty,' said Charlie firmly.

'Oh, bit I'm sorry sir, ye were deein sixty, onywye.'

'Forty,' repeated Charlie.

'And I'm tellin ye sixty.'

Mary leaned across. 'Oh, for ony sake, officer, dinna argy wi him fin he's been drinkin.'

IN 1974, just before the last local-government reorganisation, households in places where boundary changes were likely were sent explanations from the Scottish Office as to what was being proposed, how it would affect them and also inviting representations.

At one out-of-the-way farm in the Cabrach, the son of the house took the letter to his elderly mother and read it out to her. She listened closely, without saying anything. When he had finished, she thought deeply for a few minutes.

'So fit dis it bile doon til?' she asked.

'Well,' said the son, 'fae fit I understand, we winna be in Banffshire efter next year, we'll be in Moray District.'

'I see,' mused his mother.

'Bit it says here that if we wint ti complain, we should write til this address.'

'I see.'

'So will we complain?'

'No, no, we'll jist leave it. I couldna thole anither Banffshire winter.'

ELSIE WAS happily married to Bert and they had five children. Then Bert died. Shortly, Elsie married Dod, and they had four children. Then Dod died. Before long, Elsie married Chae and they had five children. Then Chae died. Not long after, Elsie died.

At her funeral, friends filed past the casket, and one lady murmured: 'See foo nice Elsie looks in her goon, and isn't it nice they they're together again?'

The woman behind her asked: 'Fa div ye mean? Elsie and Bert?'

'No,' said the woman.

'Well, ye mean Elsie and Dod?'

'No.'

'Elsie and Chae?'

'No,' said the lady. 'I mean her knees.'

WHEN AN Aberdeen woman gave birth to triplets, the story was reported in the Press and Journal, and a medical expert interviewed explained that it was still a rare occurrence and happened probably only once in 20,000 times.

'Michty,' said one reader to another. 'I'm amazed she'd ony time for her hoosework.'

AT ONE Aberdeen Airport open day, a flying club from down south was offering pleasure flights in a World War I biplane and was doing a roaring trade, despite the fact that, as the day wore on, the wind was getting stronger and stronger.

Last in the queue were a farmer from New Pitsligo and his wife. By the time their shottie came round, the wind was really quite strong. 'It's up to you,' said the pilot. 'Air Traffic Control says we're OK for the moment, but I have to warn you that it will be quite bumpy. You won't be frightened?'

'Michty, nivver a fleg,' said the farmer. 'I'm a fairmer fae Pitsliga wi a big overdraft at the bunk. There's nae nithing can scare the likes o' me. Dee yer warst. Bit if it's gaun ti be really bumpy, we'd be due a special price, I'm thinkin.'

The pilot said he would cut his usual price of £30 to £10. Then, to add a little piquancy to the proceedings, said that the special price would apply only if the farmer was able not to scream or shout throughout the whole of the flight. The farmer accepted the challenge readily.

Not wanting to lose the £20 difference, the pilot put the plane through the worst of the windy weather, and then tried a few aerobatics, with spirals, rolls and loop-the-loops.

But the farmer said nary a word throughout it all.

When they taxied back to their part of the airport apron, the pilot helped the farmer out and accepted the £10 note that was offered.

'Well,' said the pilot. 'I must say I admire your cool. I certainly wouldn't have expected you to be able to stay quiet through all of that.'

'Weel,' said the farmer, 'I will admit I near said something fin the wife fell oot.'

IN THE days when the sleeper service south was used far more than it is now, it was a regular occurrence for the sleeping-car attendants to be asked to rouse passengers in time to get off at a particular stop.

One October evening, a sales rep boarded the train at the Joint Station, Aberdeen, and went immediately to find the attendant to impress upon him the importance of being in Berwick the following morning and told him that no matter how fast asleep he was the attendant was to kick him off the train, if necessary.

In the morning, the sales rep awoke to find himself in King's Cross, London. He went to find the attendant and the language he used was bluer than a Rangers shirt.

When his fury finally died and he stamped off, the attendant's supervisor came round and asked what all that had been about. 'I've never heard language from a passenger like that in all my career,' he said.

'That's nithing,' said the attendant. 'Ye should hiv heard the mannie I threw aff at Berwick.'

FINALLY, THERE s no truth in the rumour that when Robbie Shepherd found an old bottle of cough mixture in the bathroom cabinet, he sent his son, Gordon, out in his pyjamas to play in the sna.

Glossary

A gentleman's guide to Doric as she is spak

Acquant	Familiar
Aenoo	Just now
Aetin	Eating
Affrontit, black	Ashamed, embarrassed
Aneth	Beneath, below
Athoot	Without
Aye-aye, min	Hullo there, good fellow
Bannocks	Large, thin pancakes
Ben	Through
Bide	Stay
Birstled	Burned, sizzled
Boddim	Bottom
Bosie	Embrace, hug, cuddle
Bree	Liquid residue
Claik	Gossip
Clappit	Clapped, patted
Clart	Slap on to excess (v.)
Clart	Farmyard manure, slurry (n.)
Climmed	Climbed
Contermacious	Awkward, deliberately difficult
Coorse	Bad, coarse
Coup	Tip, topple, empty out

Craiters	Creatures
Crochlie	Infirm, unsure of step
Damn the linth	(mild expletive)
Dirlin	Rattling, ringing
Dockens	Dock leaves, a tenacious weed
Dominie	Headmaster (usu. male)
Doon aboot the mou	Depressed, out of sorts
Dother	Daughter
Dowp	Backside, posterior (anat.)
Dyeucks	Ducks
Ee	You
Eese	Use
Efterhin	Afterwards
Eyn	End
Fash	Bother, upset
Ficher	Fiddle, interfere (v.)
Fit's Adee	What's wrong?
Flechy	Infested with parasites
Fleg	Fright
Footer	Fiddle, nuisance, waste of time
Forrit	Forward
Fusslin	Whistling
Futret	Weasel or stoat (not a ferret). Now usually derogatory

Gad sakes!	Yeuch! (exclam.)
Gadgie	Chap, fellow
Ganzie	Sweater, cardigan
Gaur	Make
Gey	Quite, really
Grieve	Farmworker's foreman
Gulshach	Sweets
Gype	Idiot, poltroon (usu. male)
Hairst	Harvest
Hale	Whole
Hinder end	End (taut.) pron. 'hinner'
Hirply	Hobbly, unsteady
Ilky	Each
Ill-natered	Not of sunny disposition (usu. married female)
Ingin	Onion
Intimmers	Insides (anat.)
Ivnoo	Now, at this moment
Jaloose	To reckon or fathom
Jinkin	Ducking and diving, chicaning
Jints	Joints (anat.)
Keekin	Looking impishly
Kirn-up	Mess
Kittle up	Enliven, invigorate

Kniv-fae	Fistful
Loon	Boy
Losh be here!	My goodness! (exclam.)
Loup	Jump
Mairriet	Wed, married, betrothed
Mischanter	Mishap
Mochey	Grey, drab, dreary
Neuk	Corner
News	Chat, discussion (n.)
Nickum	Imp, mischief-maker
Oots and ins	Kirby grips, hairpins
Orraloon	Young farm labourer
Ower the heid	A surfeit, in excess
Pints	Laces
Plooky	Pock-marked, enjoying a surfeit of pimples
Plottin	Sweating
Poodin	Best part of any meal
Priggin wi	Pleading with
Puckle	A few
Pucklie	Small amount of
Pyokie	Small bag containing something
Quaet	Quiet, peaceful
Quine	Girl

Riggit	Ready (usu. sartorial)
Rikkin	Smoking, steaming
Rive	Rip, tear or wrench
Roost	Rust
Rooze	To anger, inflame
Rowin	Transporting (also wrapping)
Saat	Salt
Sair	Sore, painful
Sair-made	Troubled, in pain
Scuddlin	Idling, lazing (usu. while sartorially challenged)
Semmit	Vest
Sharn	Slurry (usu. agricultural)
Sheen	Shoes
Shooed	Sewed, sewn
Sikkin	Needing, requiring
Siller	Money, cash
Skirlie	North-east delicacy, best with onions slightly burned
Skite	Slide
Skitter	Diarrhoea
Slubber	To slurp (onom.)
Snod	In good order
Sookit-lookin	Puckered, wrinkled (usu. corpses or accountants)

Soss	Mess
Sotter	Mess
Spad	Spade
Speir	Ask
Spew	Vomit
Spile	Spoil, damage
Spunks	Matches, lucifers
Stairvin	Freezing
Stappit	Rammed, jammed, forced
Stots	Bounces
Strae-ricks	Straw stacks
Styter	Stumble, stagger
Sup	Small amount (usu. liquid)
Swack	Supple, fit
Sweir	Reluctant (adj.)
Sweir	Swear (v.)
Teem	Empty
Tekkie	Outing, trip, visit
Toonsers	Indigenes of Aberdeen (derog.)
Trachled	Troubled, worn out, exhausted
Trock	Rubbish, debris, garbage (usu. concrete n., not abstract)
Trumpin	Tramping
Twa pun	Two pounds (weight)

Tyauve	Struggle (pron. 'chaav')
Vratch	wretch
Waur nor	Worse than
Weerin	Wearing
Wheen	Good few
Wheepit	Whipped
Widin	Wading
Wrang spy	Mistaken identity
Wyte	Fault
Wytin	Waiting
Wyve	Weave
Yestreen	Previous evening
Yokie	Itchy
Yokin	Starting work

Where Credit's Due

AS WE said in the Foreword, we can't claim all the glory for the tales you have read here. This book wouldn't be as full and varied as it is without the help of the many people who took the time and trouble to write down their favourite family stories, professional stories, schoolday stories and chance eavesdropping stories and sent them to us. We are exceptionally grateful, and the least we can do is record their contribution. If we have missed anyone out, we're sorry.

Thanks to Esma Shepherd, Alison Harper, Jack from Kincorth, Les Wheeler, Frances Patterson, Peter Nicol, Andy Duff, Norman Connell, Jack Kellas, Mrs M. Robertson, Peggy Veitch, Sandy Mackie, Margaret Ross, Major Rory Haugh, Leslie Innes, Joyce Everill, James Stewart, A. Gill, Ian Middleton from Arradoul, Alistair Ross, Hamish Mair, Johnnie Duncan, T. Munro Forsyth, Geordie Stott, V.B. Taylor, R.P. Nicol, A.J. Harper, Norman Harper sen., Isabel Ford, Bill McCormick, Nancy Forsyth, Ogilvie Thomson, Bryan Smith, Chris Clark, Gordon Argo, Ron Anderson, Eric Stevenson, Bill Duguid, Ethel Simpson, Mary Kennedy, Margaret Black, Nan Sandison, G.E. Smart, Douglas Mutch, Lilianne Grant Rich, Ray McIntosh, Edwin Reid, Mary Campbell, Carolyn Smith, Rena Gaiter, Mrs L. Christie, Ron Knox, Alec Cameron, Gordon Milne, Eileen McHardy, Miss B.H. Ritchie, P. Dawson, Willie J. Taylor, P.J. Duncan, Helen Walker, Graham MacLennan, Chrissie Sutherland, Chrissabel Reid, John Stewart, Frances Jaffray, Sandy Watt, Lorna Alexander, Sybil Copeland, Aileen Jason, Sandy Mustard, Evelyn Leslie and dozens of others who wrote and requested anonymity, as well as thousands who, over the years, have entertained each of us with their conversation.

Norman Harper and Robbie Shepherd
Aberdeen, 1995

And Finally . . .

A sequel is in the planning stages already. If you know of a classic example of North-east humour – true stories only, please – do write to us. If you seek anonymity, it's guaranteed, but we don't want your stories to go to waste.

Drop us a line at: Dash o' the Doric,
                                  Canongate Books Ltd.,
                                  14 High Street,
                                  Edinburgh
                                  EH1 1TE